GROW THROUGH DISRUPTION

Breakthrough Mindsets to
Innovate, Change and
Win with the OGI

Brett Richards

London | New York

Published by Clink Street Publishing 2017

Copyright © 2017

First edition.

The author asserts the moral right under the Copyright, Designs and Patents Act 1988 to be identified as the author of this work.

All rights reserved. No part of this publication may be reproduced, stored in a retrieval system or transmitted, in any form or by any means without the prior consent of the author, nor be otherwise circulated in any form of binding or cover other than that with which it is published and without a similar condition being imposed on the subsequent purchaser.

Graphic credits:

Thangka: OceanFishing, File #: 465788032, Thinkstock.com

Celtic cross: icefront, File #: 148973578, Thinkstock.com

Geometric abstract: berya113, File #: 513317456, Thinkstock.com

ISBN:
978-1-912262-47-2 - paperback
978-1-912262-48-9 - ebook

Contents

FOREWORD IX

PREFACE XIII

ACKNOWLEDGEMENTS XIX

CHAPTER 1: SEEING THE INVISIBLE 1

When maximizing organizational growth, it's the things we can't see that matter most. Leaders are asked to think differently about ways to improve their organization's ability to create new value and to change more effectively, but few have the tools to set them up for success. Here we'll explore this common shortcoming and begin to lift the veil.

CHAPTER 2: WINNING *IS* EVERYTHING 21

In professional sports, winning or being first is everything. In business, "winning" is critical for success — but does it always mean being first? Winning within organizations is more complex and is dependent on many factors, including its vision, mission, strategy, and values. We'll reveal what the most successful organizations consider when developing their winning strategies.

CHAPTER 3: MINDSETS MATTER 41

Organizational mindsets are deeper than corporate climate and are a tangible expression of an organization's culture. After the distinction of mindsets is explored, we'll introduce the 4 Principal Mindsets under which every organization falls.

CHAPTER 4: WHAT'S YOUR ORGANIZATION'S MINDSET? 57

A new model demonstrates the link between the 4 Principal Mindsets and the four core organizational types. The characteristics that organizations inherently value ultimately shape their evolution. Given mindsets are an expression of an organization's underlying values, beliefs and cognitive preferences, they can be linked to various organizational types. We'll explore the traits of each one, and will highlight how to manage the associated risks and rewards.

CHAPTER 5: THE TRANSFORMATION WHEEL® 73

Change and transformation are at the root of growth. This chapter describes the 8 Orientations that influence an organization's capability for growth and its readiness for change, and explores key factors that influence an organization's ability to do so adaptively.

CHAPTER 6: MEASURING SHIFTS IN ORGANIZATIONAL MINDSETS 99

It is now possible to tangibly track shifts in your organization's mindset to gauge the extent to which your organization is achieving positive change. We'll take a look at how an academic institution was successful in shifting strategically toward a more creative and entrepreneurial mindset.

CHAPTER 7: MEASURING SHIFTS IN AN ORGANIZATION'S GROWTH MINDSET 109

How a mid-sized, family-run company tracked shifts in its transformational "readiness" and growth mindset over a three-year period.

CHAPTER 8: GLOBAL COMPANIES IMPROVING GROWTH CAPABILITY WITH THE OGI® 117

With the OGI Scoring Index, companies can connect their OGI results to their actual revenue growth rates. This chapter explores case study applications of three large-scale companies that leveraged the OGI to support their growth mandates.

CHAPTER 9: LEADERSHIP STYLES TO SHIFT ORGANIZATIONAL MINDSETS 133

Leaders are integral to organizational success, but it's not always possible to tangibly quantify the extent to which they influence an organization's ability to grow and transform. In this chapter, we'll tangibly demonstrate how different leadership styles directly affect an organization's ability to fulfill its vision for growth.

CHAPTER 10: GETTING STARTED WITH THE OGI 143

Insight and understanding are critical ingredients for growth, but their effects are lost without transforming their power into intelligent action. In this chapter, we explore six key questions and five practical steps you can take to accelerate growth and improve your organization's performance.

APPENDIX A 149

An overview of the OGI's statistical properties.

INDEX 155

Foreword

We live in a world where change is everywhere, constant and ongoing. It is not merely changes in technology or regulatory systems and political leadership, but demographics, social attitudes, economic shifts, climate change, and other transformations. Historically, it has always been so. However, in the last decades, we have seen an emphasis on how uncertain and unpredictable these changes have become. Words and phrases like "Black Swans" and "VUCA" are now firmly implanted in the management lexicon. With this has come new emphasis on organizational adaption in the ability to grow and thrive in this disruptive and disrupting world.

With this emphasis on change and adaptability has come much literature on this topic and the pressure it places on leadership. While many leadership programs are good and have immense value, their effects are limited unless there is systematic follow up and reinforcement. The equation of Leadership + Training = Improved Organizational Performance is not wrong, but as Dr. Richards points out, it is not sufficient. In his work, it needs to be:

$$\text{Organization System + Leadership + Training =}$$
$$\text{Improved Organization Performance}$$

Much of the previous work on organization culture, change, and leadership has tended to address specific and often isolated activities and/or departments. Too often, talent, HR or personnel issues have been addressed separately from the core Vision, Mission, Goals, Strategy, Culture, and Operations of the whole organization. Too often the strategic mindset has been too narrow or too focused on improving performance in a "present" environment, rather than building towards the new and emerging environment. In other words, much of the work, while valid in and of itself, has not been integrated, adaptive, systematic, or systematically measured.

Following the lead of systems thinking, Dr. Richards conceives of organizations as being cognitive systems, and like all growing biological or electro-mechanical systems, have feedback loops that are measured and acted upon. These cognitive systems or mindsets need to be understood both in their organizational totality, as well as the component managerial and operational activities.

Dr. Richards asks that we research and understand the mindset biases of our organizations and its people and use this knowledge to assess how ready or able we are to make needed changes to thrive in this ever-disruptive world. Importantly, he asks us to use this analysis in improving the skills and capabilities of our people in their training and talent development planning. His Organizational Growth Indicator (OGI®) is, as he says, both a descriptor and an ability measure to help us understand the mindset biases of our organization, and a goal and tracking mechanism for training and talent development.

This is one of the many major contributions of this work. Not only will it help organizations discover the mindset biases that hinder growth in their culture, structure and talent development practices, but integrating the OGI measures into what he calls The Transformation Wheel indicates how the organization can make needed changes and develop those feedback loops.

Measures of training effectiveness in both the US and Canada cast doubt on the success of many training programs, especially leadership programs. In the 2015 Canadian Conference Board survey, only 29 percent of their respondents rated their leadership development programs effective. However, avoidance of training is not the solution. According to global productivity and innovation surveys done by both IMD and INSEAD, the US and Canada have been reducing their commitment to management education and training and are seeing the negative results in measures of productivity and innovation. Countries like China and India are stepping up their activity and are experiencing positive results.

The answer is not to walk away from training and development, but to set it in a measurable systematic organizational context. As Dr. Richards shows in both his models and case studies, the answer is to set talent development and training in the context of an understanding of his 4 Principal Mindsets and his 8 Orientations. By using the research and analysis that results from systematic application of his OGI and Transformation Wheel, organizations will not only be able to improve the effectiveness and ROI of their talent development budgets, but will position themselves much better to continue growth in this "Black Swan"/"VUCA"/disruptive global environment.

Alan Middleton, PhD
Executive Director Schulich Executive Education Centre
Schulich School of Business, York University, Canada
2017

Preface

What does it mean to "grow through disruption"? A premise of this book is that the waves of change are not going to subside anytime soon. What other option do we have other than to find ways to cope with what seems to be perpetual tsunami-type waves coming at us from tectonic shifts occurring in virtually every aspect of our lived experience?

We are told that with change comes opportunity. However, opportunity can only be realized with the right mindset. In sessions I run with leadership teams, I often ask, "What kind of a mindset and disposition is required to 'embrace ambiguity, uncertainty, and change' rather than merely suffer through it kicking and screaming?"

In this book, I'll be introducing 4 Principal Mindsets that are essential for organizations and leaders to embrace in order to grow and sustain future success through disruption. The first step is to diagnose and understand what mindsets your leaders and organization are currently utilizing the most. The second step is to explore where they need to shift — what mindsets will be required for your leaders and organization to master if they are to successfully adapt to current and emergent change. The third step, for my pragmatic readers, is finding practical ways to effectively grow through disruption.

Understandably, the word disruption is being thrown around quite a bit these days and for good reason. By "disruption," I mean the type of change that is so profound it shatters our current assumptions and compels us to reconstruct our ways of thinking if we are to thrive successfully into the future. Disruption, then, is not your normal run-of-the-mill type of change. It is far more intense and urgent, brought about by highly turbulent and increasingly complex environments, not unlike what we are currently experiencing right now socially, politically, and economically.

Clayton Christensen's and later, Michael Raynor's, notion of "disruption" is not lost in this context*. In brief, these thought leaders describe disruption as a distinct theory and approach to innovation, characterized by an intentional strategy to offer a different value proposition to customers. Disruptive innovations typically introduce lower-performing products at a lower cost to compete against mainstream products that are currently available on the market. Over time, these initially inferior products improve in quality and scope, eroding the market share of mainstream incumbents, and eventually disrupting (if not destroying) legacy products and business models.

The call to action for currently successful organizations is to take disruption theory very seriously by actively seeking ways to sustain growth and survival by challenging traditional ways of thinking and ways of offering new value to their customers.

When I speak of growth, I'm referring to individual and organizational learning, performance, and results. At the individual leader level, disruption necessitates responsive action. Our intent and desire to respond well requires thinking and emotional agility. The cyclic process of adaptation — observing, interpreting, assimilating, and responding — presents countless opportunities for learning if we are open and receptive to it. That is, if we have the right mindset. Is it even possible to successfully adapt to disruption without learning to think, feel, and act differently?

I will propose in this book that organizations are in fact *cognitive systems* that I believe have profound implications for understanding how organizations attempt to grow amidst high levels of disruption in their operating environments. Organizations, as *cognitive systems*, also observe their environments, selecting, interpreting and acting on data, information, and knowledge in their adaptive efforts. Now with the advent of cognitive computing, artificial intelligence (AI) and the Internet of Things, my premise that organizations are in fact *cognitive systems* becomes more prescient.

The world is getting smarter and organizations need to get smarter with it. I suggest organizations are "intelligent" to the extent that they are able to learn and adapt in such a way that allows them to achieve their purpose and succeed within a given domain.

---

* See Clayton Christensen, *The Innovator's Dilemma*; Christensen and Raynor, *The Innovator's Solution*; and Raynor, *The Innovator's Manifesto*.

From this vantage point, cognition and cognitive capability become critically important topics for organizations. It is my hope that you find within this book some new ideas related to knowing and understanding your organization as a cognitive system and, more importantly, find practical methods to improve your organization's ability to grow through disruption. Increasing your organization's cognitive, innovative, and transformative capabilities is the essential ingredient to achieve intelligent action and win in the new age of intelligence.

> *"Now more than ever before,*
> *leaders need to take the guesswork out of driving growth*
> *with better metrics to identify the previously hidden,*
> *yet vital factors influencing their organization's ability*
> *to create new value and change — adaptively."*

Within the context of an increasingly complex, disruptive environment, senior leaders in organizations of every kind need advanced tools to help them make smarter decisions, particularly related to improving their organization's ability to grow through innovation and adaptive change. Another core objective of this book, then, will be to present a valid and practical diagnostic tool, called the OGI®, for leaders to identify both their organization's strengths, and, critically, the previously hidden factors that are constraining their organization's growth capability.

The OGI (Organizational Growth Indicator) is a vital tool for every business leader. No matter your industry or the size of your company, the OGI is capable of giving you invaluable insight into the inner workings of your organization. Any executive wanting to drive growth, innovation, and positive transformation in disruptive environments will need to start with a clear and accurate assessment of their organization. This is what the OGI provides: tangible metrics to take the guesswork out of driving innovation, growth, and sustained success both locally and globally.

Re-thinking Organizational Improvement

Ultimately, the purpose of the OGI is to support lasting organizational improvement and performance. Too often, organizational improvement efforts are directed exclusively toward developing leaders. Significant investments in time and dollars are spent focused on developing leadership skills deemed essential to improving organizational performance and results. No doubt, leaders are integral to supporting organizational success, and there are many top-notch leadership skills development programs. The challenge is selecting the right programs, with the right leaders, where improvement is most needed within the system to improve organizational performance and results.

The current organizational performance equation seems to be:

$$\text{Leaders + Training = Improved Organizational Performance}$$

The problem with this equation is that leaders are required to enact their new-found skills within the broader organizational system. If the system doesn't offer the right supporting conditions, then leaders will be unable to fully leverage their new-found skills, and the organization will not maximize its return on investment (ROI) on the training investment it has made. No wonder many CEOs are left feeling unsatisfied with the results, or lack of results, of many leadership development programs. At best, the effects of a great training program are short-lived, largely because the organization itself has somehow been removed from the equation designed to do just that: improve organizational performance.

If the goal is to truly improve organizational performance and results, I would suggest a different performance equation:

$$\text{Organizational System + Leaders + Training =}$$
$$\text{Improved Organizational Performance}$$

For whatever reason, the fact that organizations are systems has been missed. Going back to the beginning of my research journey, the OGI was developed with the mindset that organizations are systems, cognitive systems in fact. It was and remains my view that this matters tremendously if you are truly interested in identifying an organization's actual ability to innovate and change, or if you are interested in shifting your organization's mindset to be more innovative and entrepreneurial.

Without a tangible, objective understanding of the organizational system, decision makers run the risk of flying blind. They might go ahead and implement training programs that, on the surface, seem to fit but will likely prove ineffective given underlying dynamics at play within the organizational system. Case in point: one client organization lamented the fact that they spent significant training dollars on a creativity skill development program in an effort to boost the organization's ability to innovate, but the program had virtually no lasting effect. Despite being a good program in its own right, it had little real impact because "the organization" was left out of the organizational performance equation. Throwing training at a problem without understanding the organizational system will often lead to unsatisfactory results, not to mention misspent resources.

Intent of the OGI – Lasting Organizational Improvement

Your organization can leverage the quantitative results found within the OGI analysis to:

1. pinpoint areas that are supporting and/or constraining your organization's current capability and future potential,
2. select specific areas that will offer the greatest impact to accelerate and improve your organization's capability, maximizing return on effort and dollars,
3. develop targeted strategies/actions, programs/training custom designed to improve your organization's transformative capability,
4. execute on those select activities, and
5. quantitatively track, evaluate, and fine tune your organization's progress to higher levels of innovative and transformative capability year-over-year.

I founded Connective Intelligence almost twenty years ago. My focus as an organizational development practitioner and later also as an "applied" researcher has been to ignite the performance and potential of leaders and their organizations. The interplay between leaders and the organizational system in which they work is perhaps what fascinates me the most. This book is a response, as much as it is a call to action.

It's a response in the sense that it is increasingly difficult for leaders to formulate adaptive organizations capable of thriving and growing during high volatility and uncertainty. As an organization development practitioner, I saw a big void in valid, quantitative tools available for leaders to use that are specifically focused on improving their organization's innovative and transformative capability. Leaders are typically given some form of engagement survey tool, which is useful in its own right. However, it is not designed to assess an organization's ability to grow through new value creation and adaptive change. The OGI is.

This book is a call to action in the sense that I'm encouraging leaders to challenge themselves to think differently about their organizations, if they wish to grow their organizations through disruption. Systems thinking is required. With the OGI, leaders can see how the whole organization is responding to the factors within the system influencing its ability to grow.

Brett Richards

Acknowledgements

The ideas proposed in this book have sprung from my interactions and learnings with so many great minds in academia and business over the years to whom I am deeply indebted. This book is an evolution of my doctoral dissertation, so I would be remiss not to thank my committee. Dr. Bob Silverman, enriched my thinking in so many ways, notably through hours of dialogue pertaining to the nature of organizations, and their quadratic structure. Drs. Fred Steier, Rich Appelbaum and Carina Fiedeldey-Van Dijk each offered rich perspectives related to systems theory, organizational effectiveness and the development of statistically sound assessments.

Many thanks go to Jerry Rhodes and his remarkable system of Effective Intelligence which has shaped my thinking beyond measure over the last twenty years, particularly related to cognitive styles and his unique conceptualization of thinking-intentions. Thanks also to Bob Wiele, a great, early mentor of mine whose intellect and creativity left an indelible impression on me and my approach to learning and development. I was fortunate to study with the late Sensei Miguel Palavecino, a master martial artist in the truest sense of the word, who introduced me to Tai Chi, the practice of mindfulness, intentional action and the important integration of mind-body-spirit. My deep gratitude goes to the late Bishop Henry Hill who embodied what it means to be a truly spiritual being. He had a deep intellect with an even deeper faith in God and the goodness that rests within all of us.

Related to the nitty-gritty task of getting the book done I would like to thank Daina Astwood-George for her fresh thinking and pragmatic sensibility. A dear colleague of mine, author Martin Rutte, founder of Project Heaven on Earth once said to me: "No David, no book, no kidding." He was right. I'm grateful to David Christel for the many hours he committed to this book. I would not have accomplished it without him. Most of all, I appreciated David's sharp mind blended with a gentle spirit which offers a rare mix indeed.

My team at Connective Intelligence must be thanked as I'd never get any project completed, book or otherwise, without their commitment and support.

I dedicate this book to my children, Courtney, Kyle and James who never cease to amaze, and to Lois, my wife and greatest inspiration of all. Thank you for blessing my life with yours.

The following are some *Inconvenient Truths* I've uncovered related to innovation within organizations. They are inconvenient because they are things that require attention and acknowledgment even though they may be difficult to do or accept. We may even choose to ignore or deny their existence, however, doing so may lessen the impact of our efforts at accelerating organizational growth through innovation and adaptive change.

You will see them pop up throughout the book. Any look familiar? There are likely more.

Inconvenient Truths

1. Leaders of organizations need better ways to measure, quantify, and demystify innovation so that it can be tangibly addressed in a systematic way.

2. Innovation is a leading indicator of an organization's ability to sustain future success.

3. The majority of organizations still view innovation as a "nice to have" not a "need to have," and they eventually pay the price. Those that do value and see the need for innovation struggle with how to do it well, or better.

4. The goals of organizations and the goals of innovation are most often the same and yet the two are experienced by organizational members as enemies, not allies.

5. Creativity is absolutely essential, but it's not the whole story.

6. An inability to break the bonds of short-term thinking at the leadership level will kill innovation.

7. Organizations are most often adept at short-term, incremental innovation, but are typically much less effective at long-term, transformative, or radical forms of innovation.

8. Failing to understand the full ramifications of the fact that organizations are complex systems, rather than a collection of complicated processes, will severely constrain an organization's transformational potential — their ability to initiate and sustain innovation.

9. There is no innovation without leadership support.

10. There is a dramatic need to better understand the relationship between organizational thinking and organizational innovation.

11. Effective organizations are most likely to be successful with innovation and yet it's the ineffective organizations that need it most and who often experience numerous failed innovation attempts, a.k.a. the vicious cycle.

12. Engagement surveys are useful, but not substantive enough to fully grasp, describe, and enable how to improve organizational innovation and transformation.

13. Innovation and transformation are every bit as emotional as intellectual for every member of an organization.

CHAPTER 1

SEEING THE INVISIBLE

*"The seeds of decline are usually in place
long before decline becomes visible —
like a disease where you look strong on the outside,
but you're already ill on the inside."*

Getting a Grip on Reality

For millennia, philosophers have searched to understand the nature of reality. How is reality described, how is it known and how does it influence the happiness and success we experience in our lives? We hear and make references to "reality" all the time using phrases like: "the reality is…"; or "wow, what planet are they on?"; or "man, are they out of touch…"; and more recently the notion of "fake news," which is, of course, another way of saying that what you are reading is false and out of touch with "reality."

Reality is not just something that is tangible, that we can visibly see with our eyes; it is also something we *feel* or *experience*. In other words, the stuff of reality — facts — takes on two primary forms: they can be drawn from the tangible, objective, external world; or they can be drawn from the intangible realm of hidden, subjective impressions and opinions.

Now this is not a book about philosophy or the nature of reality *per se*, but it is a book that attempts to help leaders, managers, co-workers, and all members of an organization understand and "see" both the tangible and invisible facts, and indeed forces, at play within their own organizations. The hidden facts — those that are not easily observable — are every bit as "real" in that they influence the experience of organizational members, as well as shape the decisions, actions, and results that organizations get.

Inconvenient Truth #1
Leaders of organizations need better ways to measure, quantify, and demystify innovation so that it can be tangibly addressed in a systematic way.

The challenge for all organizations — be they commercially focused, not-for-profit, governmental, academic, artistic, or scientific — is not just about their leaders finding new ways to be aware of and observe subtle realities, but to also find new ways for them to absorb and accurately interpret the emergent signals of significance that arise and are available for responsive action. Below is just a small sample of organizations that either misread or failed to respond adaptively to the signals of change.

Blockbuster Video	Sharper Image
Fashion Café	Washington Mutual Bank
CBGB	Enron
The Hit Factory	WorldCom
SwissAir	Polaroid
Woolworth's	Atkins Nutritionals
Bre-X Minerals	Bethlehem Steel
Borders	White Star Lines (Titanic)
IndyMac	Commodore Computers
Edison Records	Pan Am

A greater appreciation of the dance between both types of realities at play — tangible vs. intangible — within organizations is crucial knowledge for leaders to draw upon, particularly those interested in driving innovation, stimulating growth, and achieving long-term viability for their organizations.

What's the Current Reality of Your Organization?

Having a sound understanding of the current reality of your organization is essential. Most leaders intuitively feel they have a pretty good sense as to where their organization is at with respect to performance, growth, value, strength, and sustainability. But do they really? What information about their organization are they potentially missing? Are there any hidden realities — facts — at play that could be silently damaging the long-term health and survival of their organization? Take a look at the following table.

Where is your organization now? Where does it need to be?

OGI Growth & Transformation Tier Rating	Tier 5	Tier 4	Tier 3	Tier 2	Tier 1
OGI Overall Scoring Range – %	≥66%	65 – 57%	56 – 48%	47 – 39%	≤38%
Overall "Stance" to the Operating Environment	Pre-emptive	Proactive	Mixed	Reactive	Non-responsive
Ability to Grow through New Value Creation	Advanced	Proficient	Moderate	Marginal	Poor
Ability to Effectively Change	Excelling	Thriving	Adapting	Developing	Lagging

This is known as the OGI (Organizational Growth Indicator) Scoring Index. Where is your company or organization on this: Tier 5, Tier 1, or a mash-up of all the tiers? Where do you feel you need to be to not only satisfy your organization's mission, vision and goals, but be a leader in your industry, while maintaining high employee satisfaction, creativity, loyalty, and innovation ratings?

Right now, you likely don't have a diagnostic tool to really help you discern and definitively *know* just where your company is at, related to its ability to grow through new value creation and adaptive change. What you need to know is the actual *reality* of your company's ability to achieve intelligent action and win in our fast-changing, disruptive world.

Growing through disruption requires three fundamental activities for leaders interested in improving organizational innovation and enhancing their readiness for change: first, a deeper, holistic understanding of the current state or "reality" of their organization; second, a clear plan of action to shift the organization's mindset in line with its vision and strategic requirements; and third, a method to annually track, evaluate, and fine tune efforts used to drive growth and organizational improvement.

The OGI offers leaders an incisive, practical diagnostic that tunes into and quantifies both the visible and previously invisible qualities and facts influencing an organization's overall capability and capacity to adapt. Painting a more comprehensive description and understanding of the true state or environment of an organization provides leaders with an opportunity to more proactively address the constraints that will prevent growth and long-term success.

Inconvenient Truth #2
Innovation is a leading indicator of an organization's ability to sustain future success.

Without the kind of diagnostic power that the OGI offers to measure an organization's true reality, the hidden "seeds of decline" may go unaddressed and evolve into a virus that permeates the whole organization, eventually strangling its vitality and ability to sustain itself.

In an interview with Jim Collins titled, "How Mighty Companies Fail,"[1] he indicates there are three important things to keep in mind related to the demise of previously great companies, all of which are relevant to the theme and force of this book. First and foremost, Collins states: It's very difficult to fix things we cannot see or that fall outside of our awareness.

The power of the OGI (Organizational Growth Indicator) is very simple: *it's a practical diagnostic tool that sheds light on previously hidden dynamics affecting an organization's growth capability.* As with anything, the power of any new diagnostic tool is that it allows us to *see things that were previously unknown to us*, setting the foundation for new thinking and knowledge to occur.

Throughout history, science has shown us the power of this. Using the new observational tools available to them in their era:

- Copernicus and Galileo helped people to see that our world is not flat, nor is it the centre of the universe, as was previously believed for centuries.
- Through deep observation and experimentation, Heisenberg, Einstein and others uncovered the subatomic, quantum world, cracking open

the foundational laws of Newtonian mechanics, which had informed the way we viewed and understood our universe for hundreds of years.

- X-Rays, discovered in 1895 by Wilhelm Conrad Röntgen, were once the only non-invasive way to look inside the inner workings of our bodies. They are still useful to look at bone structure, but they aren't nearly as effective as MRIs or ultrasounds when it comes to exploring the soft tissue and organs within our bodies. With just an X-Ray, our bodies may appear to be healthy and vibrant even though our livers or hearts are diseased.

More refined diagnostics enable deeper levels of observation, which help us to see more things and, importantly, help us to repair and act on things that could potentially harm us over the long term if left undetected. Most of us, when going to our family physician or specialist, expect them to offer the latest developments in technology in order to identify the root causes of our ailments, especially if we are experiencing adverse symptoms indicating our bodies are not functioning normally.

So if organizations are indicating symptoms of *dis-ease* — meaning they aren't growing; they aren't producing the profits or results they desire — then why wouldn't their leaders want to utilize a painless, yet highly incisive diagnostic tool to pinpoint the root causes of those issues? This is a serious question, particularly given Collins' next point in the interview.

The second point made by Collins identifies somewhat of a paradox. He states, "We tend to think decline happens because of complacency — people just sitting still, not being aggressive or innovating. But we found there's often tremendous change and innovation leading right up to the point of fall. It's overreaching: undisciplined growth, undisciplined risk-taking."

There is a definite paradox existing for many organizations, and that is to balance short-term profitability with long-term viability. The collapse of previously successful companies like Sears Roebuck, Enron, Blockbuster, Eastman Kodak, General Motors and BlackBerry, to name just a few examples, offer striking examples describing the serious effects of this paradox.

New innovative business ideas are often starved for resources simply because leaders, in their efforts to meet quarterly profit targets, cannot justify dedicating time and energy to interesting, but low margin ventures. According to one leader interviewed from Kodak, "The hot new thing simply cannot produce enough revenues this quarter to improve my bonus as a senior executive."[2]

Clayton Christensen describes this paradox as a "dilemma" that many previously successful organizations have faced. How is it that "the logical, competent decisions of management that are critical to the success of their companies are also the reasons why they lose their positions of leadership"?[3] Importantly, the demise of previously successful companies is not due to inactive or ill-intentioned leadership practices *per se*, rather they appear to be due to a systemic inability to make the necessary organizational changes required to achieve long-term viability.

*** Inconvenient Truth #3***
*The majority of organizations still view innovation
as a "nice to have" not a "need to have,"
and they eventually pay the price.
Those that do value and see the need for innovation
struggle with how to do it well, or better.*

The demise of previously successful companies unable to adapt despite the conscious if not conscientious efforts of their leadership, points to the complex dynamics at play within organizational systems. Organizations are complex systems, not just an array of complicated processes. Too often, organizations are viewed as a collection of individuals rather than complex systems consisting of interdependent elements such as, but certainly not limited to, culture, processes, structure, and leadership. Importantly, they all influence each other in non-linear ways. Consequently, just "fixing" any of these elements in isolation without paying attention to the others will lead to a lot of busy activity, but ultimately, to ineffective results for the organization.

Failure to identify and attend to these often-hidden dynamics in an effective way will eventually undermine the organization's adaptive capability. An important premise of this book, then, is that innovation must in fact be viewed as a *whole-system phenomenon*. Leaders are required to take a systems view — to think systemically, not just linearly — to accurately gauge and improve their organization's growth and adaptive capability. The OGI is an instrument intentionally grounded in systems theory and, as such, provides leaders with a lens to view their organizations systemically, shedding light on subtle yet crucial enterprise-wide dynamics previously unseen, or intentionally ignored, which, as we've seen, can prove perilous.

We cannot see how leaders think, nor can we see how they feel — not at least until we focus our attention on it. Faulty thinking and misguided emotions of the leadership will eventually be the demise of any organization. Their intentions may be pure, but without the right thinking and emotional intelligence — emotional composure and fluency — their actions will fall flat and their organizations will be in serious risk of failure.

The third and final point made by Collins in the interview speaks to the resilience of organizations and their ability to rise like a phoenix out of the ashes of defeat. He states: "I was surprised by how far you really can fall and still come back — it's one of the most wonderful things to come from this work. The tendency for many of us might be to give up too early."

Some great organizations, such as Apple and IBM, were titans that fell to the brink of disaster but were able to find a way to rise to greatness once again. Under the right leadership capable of galvanizing the hearts and minds of employees around a compelling vision, shared purpose and values, organizations are at least positioned for renewal. Importantly organizations, even very large ones, can adapt and renew. They are inherently capable of adapting to internally and/or externally generated change, which is good to know considering the amount of volatility and change we are experiencing in our world. It's a VUCA world — no matter where you go on this planet and it doesn't matter in what field of endeavour. What does VUCA stand for?

Volatility, Uncertainty, Complexity, and Ambiguity

A quick way of describing what each of these terms means is to look at their opposites.

- The opposite of *Volatility* is *Stability* — Would you say your business environment is stable?
- The opposite of *Uncertainty* is *Certainty* — Would you say that you have a good grasp on what the future holds?

- The opposite of *Complexity* is *Simplicity* — Would you say organizational life is getting simpler?
- The opposite of *Ambiguity* is *Predictability* — Would you say markets, customers, competitors, and governments are acting in predictable ways?

I think we can all agree that VUCA is an apt description of the current state of our world — it is certainly indicative of the business world and directly impacts the inner workings of organizations, which are then projected onto the world. To combat the VUCA phenomenon, we spend $130 billion annually on leadership training curriculum.[4] In the bewildering gestalt of organizational systems and methodologies — What do you go with? Who do you believe? — this is the very real context in which leaders must operate. Does it feel like VUCA is winning?

Paradoxically, living in a VUCA world demands an ability to challenge how we've known life for generations. Unfortunately, relying on solutions and approaches that worked before often fall short in our increasingly complex and ambiguous environments where predictability, drawn from past experience, is less valid.

This is a challenge for leaders because in many instances, they cannot rely on what Karl Polanyi* described as "tacit knowledge": knowledge acquired over years of experience and that informs one's ability to discern and make effective decisions.

In other words, past experience can get in the way of effective future action, which is contrary to what we always felt or declared to be true. To clarify, I am not suggesting that past experience doesn't matter. It's blind faith or an overreliance on what worked in the past — that one believes almost by default — ought to work now, which, in the future, can get leaders into trouble. To paraphrase the great German philosopher Nietzsche, what is required is the courage to challenge one's own convictions.

So, the paradox for leaders lies in needing time to learn and absorb new things — but not having the time or mental energy required to reflect in such a way that allows for real learning to occur. Shifting, modifying, and even

---

* A Hungarian-American economic historian, economic anthropologist, economic sociologist, political economist, historical sociologist, and social philosopher. Author of *The Great Transformation*.

replacing one's convictions takes thoughtful contemplation and time to bring about real learning, something many leaders don't have the luxury of.

What do I mean by "real" learning? In short, real learning implies the ability to embed new skills, attitudes, and competencies into the leader's daily practice in such a way that increases their ability to respond effectively amidst increasing levels of volatility, uncertainty, complexity, and ambiguity.

I believe this is where a key challenge lies. It's certainly not always related to the leader's willingness to learn new things because they know better than anyone else the needs they have and the challenges they face. I believe it's their ability to dedicate the time required to integrate and practice their newfound skills, given all of the urgent demands they are required to address in order to keep the daily operations of the organization moving forward.

- Leaders need to both draw on past experience and have the ability to challenge their assumptions. This requires a new habit of mind — a *shift* in mindset — which can only be embedded with practice.
- Leaders require a "both/and" mindset.
- Leaders need to balance confidence and humility. They need to both demonstrate the courage of their convictions and display an ability to receive new information, which can shift their viewpoints.

If you're in a leadership position, you may feel like you're either caught in a Catch-22 scenario of damned if you do/damned if you don't, or a never-ending loop of catching up–falling behind–catching up, etc. This leads to frustration and undermines performance at all levels in an organization, and can negatively impact customers, contractors, and vendors. Prolonged challenges can lead to desperation and desperate acts both within and beyond the company's walls.

Difficult times require different measures, which means we have to think differently. But first, we have to *see* things differently to enable new thinking and initiate more adaptive action.

The world is rapidly changing and we have to change the lens we are using to make meaning of the world emerging before our eyes. Seeing things differently can make all the difference in the world.

When it comes to truly understanding the inner workings of their organizations, however, most leaders have been flying blind for far too long and can no longer afford to do so. This is not a criticism, it's a reality given the lack of proper diagnostic tools available for leaders to take a good look inside their organizations with the level of clarity and precision required to achieve growth and sustained success in today's 21st century business environment.

While leaders cannot fully control or discern what is happening outside of their organizations, it *is* within their control to see the inner workings of their own organizations with greater clarity, leading to a more refined and effective set of actionable strategies.

In business, leaders often demonstrate a need to cut to the chase and to keep things simple. The trick is to offer solutions that are practical and easy to apply while being grounded in good theory. I'm reminded of Kurt Lewin's famous adage: "there is nothing so practical as a good theory."[5] Speaking of which —

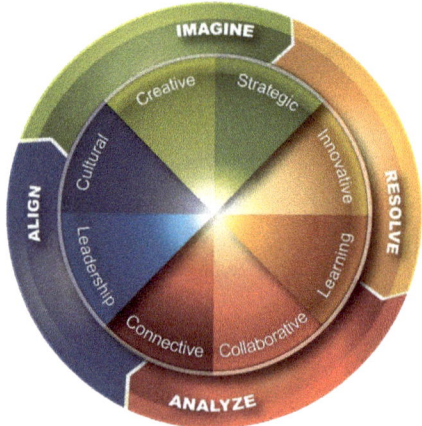

This graphic is a model representing the dimensions embedded within the OGI, the Organizational Growth Indicator. It springs from initial theory to years of research, synthesized into a practical model to help business leaders accelerate creativity, innovation, cohesiveness, focus, growth, and sustainability within their organizations.

There are many factors influencing growth within organizations, so it was no easy task to develop a user-friendly tool that did not overly simplify the complexities of organizational life. Perhaps the greatest challenge was to create a tool for business leaders that:

a. *quantified* the key factors that influence their organization's ability to grow through innovation and adaptive change, and

b. *linked* those key factors to actual performance data, such as revenue growth.

You read that right, *actual revenue growth*. In today's high-flux business environment, leaders need tangible, quantifiable metrics to validate their gut feelings and to strengthen their ability to make sound decisions. But it stands to reason that the metrics they use ought to be meaningfully connected to the actual performance of their businesses and this, I believe, is what has been sorely lacking in the field of organizational development.

Speaking the Language of Leaders

I believe that, for several reasons, leaders have historically paid too little attention to the intangible factors influencing their organization's performance: one of them has to do with language, the other has to do with the reality of business in a results-focused world. Business leaders ultimately live in a world of hard metrics and bottom-line results. If they can't easily connect the "soft" people and culture issues to tangible metrics, it's essentially not much use to them.

Too often, Human Resources (HR) and Organizational Development (OD) professionals communicate talent and engagement outcomes to business leaders in ways not clearly linked to bottom-line business results. While getting people engaged, motivated and working well together sounds great, it's often viewed as a "nice to have" but not a "need to have" when quarterly profits must be met and reported to shareholders.

Intuitively, most leaders get it: people and culture are important. In fact, 94 percent of over 722 senior executives surveyed by the *McKinsey Quarterly* indicated that people and culture were the most important drivers of innovation.[6] The challenge is that they just haven't had the means, until now, to *quantify* these seemingly invisible implicit factors and tangibly link them to "hard" metrics that drive business performance, such as revenue growth and other important key performance indicators (KPIs) relevant to their organizations. You can't see what you can't see — until it's made visible to you.

Assessing Capability for Growth

The OGI zeroes-in on twelve research-based factors — 8 Orientations and 4 Principal Mindsets — shown to influence its readiness and capability for growth. This is critical given that virtually all leaders have a mandate to ensure long-term success and to maximize customer and/or shareholder value.

The focus of leaders in many organizations is to optimize the organization's ability to stimulate growth and maximize profitability within the context of its vision, mission, values, and strategic mandate. The challenge is that most leaders focus much of their attention on *explicit* outcome measures or "effects," rather than the underlying or *implicit* "causes" that are having an, at times, dramatic effect on the organization's ability to grow and achieve desired results. The OGI is an easy-to-apply organizational diagnostic tool designed to detect underlying causes that influence an organization's ability to grow through new value creation and adaptive change.

Before we launch into the technical aspects of the OGI, let's talk a little more about organizations and this intense period of flux we're currently in.

Essentially, what's occurring is what can only be described as "epochal transformation," which sounds intense, but meaningfully highlights the epic shift in values and mindset — establishing a new epoch — in how we view people and organization, their roles, and how we cooperate in this seismic shift.

> *PROBLEM:* Like it or not, epochal transformation is more than just the buzzword of the moment, it's a reality pervading every aspect of life, including the business world. We can't afford to hang on to old ways of thinking any longer. And we can no longer afford to bury our heads in the sand in hopes that this, too, will pass. For each of us right here, right now, change is here to stay and it will not let up any time soon. How we choose to respond to continuous change is the spirit of transformation.
>
> Through transition, there's typically a high degree of tension between the needs, values, attitudes, and behaviours of the past and the emerging new order. We're still too much in the grips of mental models formulated

centuries ago. It's time to let go at a faster clip given the nature of the epochal change we're in, and the global context in which it is occurring.

The changes we are experiencing are pervasive and certainly not limited to organizational life. The entire fabric of every society across the globe is reeling from the effects of these imposing changes. As Bob Dylan, the great songwriter and poet, so aptly wailed: "…the times, they are a changin'." Truer words were never spoken.

Whether it's reeling from the effects of a global financial crisis, coping with environmental change, addressing global competition, keeping step with rapid technological change or coping with what feels like ceaseless geopolitical turmoil, we are all experiencing the effects of a world in flux on virtually every front.

On the bright side, our civilization has been through this level of change at an epic scale before. For example, some 500 years ago, around 1450, the Renaissance was kick-started in part with Gutenberg's invention of the printing press, which precipitated an explosion of information sharing and knowledge creation on a scale never before experienced.

During this momentous change "basic, common sense 'truths'" that had stood unquestioned for centuries, even millennia, were eroding away. The Earth did not stand still. The sun did not revolve around it…[and] printing boosted production of books from hundreds to millions per year."[7] As Salk and Salk point out, "These changes in our relationship to earth and to sun were changes in perception and not changes in reality; the realities were not altered, only our perception of them."[8]

Change requires us at times to shift our perspective of reality. To acknowledge that the reality we believe to be true is in fact only a version of the truth, or may even be false, as with believing the world is flat. Living through epochal change requires of us the willingness and the courage to challenge our own assumptions and beliefs about "what is real" and what is required of our collective humanity to sustain long-term success and survival.

Change, for better or worse, is something that happens, something shifts and it's no longer the same. Transformation involves a conscious intent to make adjustments or adaptations required to remain vital or to survive in response to a change. With respect to organizations and the people within them, transformation is the process of not just striving for intelligent action, but for greater resonance, vibrancy, and depth.

To get you started, let's look at organizations from a new perspective.

Perception, Meaning & Systems

How we perceive something certainly influences our sense of reality, but it also influences the meaning we obtain from it and, ultimately, apply to it. Metaphors [*meta* – over • *phora* – carry] transfer meaning from one thing to another, creating meaningful parallels between two seemingly disparate things.

Organizations have been described using various metaphors such a "machines," "brains," and "organisms" to give a few examples*. Viewing organizations using different metaphors, each with their own rationale, utility and limitations, sheds light on the marvellous variety, if not complexity, of understanding organizational life from various vantage points.

The particular lens through which we view organizations is important because it carries with it certain assumptions, if not limiting beliefs and expectations, about how organizations work, and how to fix them when they aren't working quite the way we want them to. The perspective we use to describe organizations will influence the way we think about the activities that occur within them.

Metaphors provide a useful way of thinking about organizations as if they were something else. What they don't specifically do is describe what organizations actually *are*.

In my research, I have attempted to describe what organizations are and have worked my way upwards from there to develop a new view of organizations — as cognitive systems with an underlying architecture — which has far-reaching implications for understanding how to improve and develop them through more effective innovation and organizational transformation efforts. This is what the OGI provides.

---

* See *Metaphors of Organization*, by Gareth Morgan, for an excellent account of how metaphors provide a powerful method for understanding and managing organizations.

Organizations as Systems

> *"Systems are wholes that cannot be fully understood by viewing the actions of the isolated parts that comprise them. It is the interrelationships that exist among the interacting parts that constitute the essential nature of a system."*

Organizations, as systems, are influenced by their environments and, conversely, have an effect on the environments in which they function through new or refined products, services, processes, or structures that are offered through their innovation and transformation efforts.

Perceiving organizations growing and adapting as systems requires attention to the interactions that occur among the elements within the organization, as well as the necessary relationship it has with the environment external to it.

Emery and Trist's notion of structural coupling — the interconnectedness of internal and external environments enabling them to mutually benefit each other — is particularly relevant with respect to organizational growth and transformation given that:

> "Environment and system do not just co-exist side by side. They interact to the point of mutual inter-penetration. Some aspects of the environment become 'internalized' by the system and some aspects of the system become externalized to become features of the environment."[9]

Organizations represent a particular kind of system; they may be described as open, adaptive systems. In a similar fashion, some researchers refer to organizations as "complex" adaptive systems.[10]

The adjective "complex" refers to the fact that there are "many different interacting elements" or multiple "*interactions* [occurring] in the system."[11] This is why leaders can be frustrated and somewhat perplexed when initiatives (with big price tags) intended to improve organizational results fall short.

The root cause of these kinds of failures can be traced back to a mindset that uses a set of assumptions focused on mechanistic or linear thinking rather than holistic or systems-based thinking. In short, an overreliance on short-term,

Organizations as Cognitive Systems

> *"Organizations are observing systems that attempt to make sense of their environments. The processes of observation, sense-making and intentional action are all cognitively rooted, and this is essentially why I suggest that all organizations are cognitive systems at their core."* *

An organization is a purposeful system, meaning it "can change its goals under constant conditions; it selects ends, as well as means and thus displays *will*."[12] Use of the phrase "displays will" is important because it suggests conscious, intentional choice. The ability to "change goals" implies first, a cognitive act of creation and, second, an ability to cognitively re-evaluate earlier choices, based on experience.

In addition, the ability to "select ends, as well as means" suggests an ability to cognitively monitor progress over time, toward an intentionally constructed "end" state, which implies temporal sensitivity.

Organizations as cognitive entities display intelligence.[13] To aptly suggest, then, that an organization is "purposeful" and "displays will" necessitates an underlying cognitive capacity or intelligence directed toward both the formulation and fulfillment of explicit operational and strategic objectives that are believed to support current and future success. Organizations, as cognitive systems, strive for intelligent action, meaning they are "intelligent" to the extent that they are able to "act with relevance to the maintenance [and advancement] of [themselves]."[14]

Importantly, there is a duality existing between the people working within the organization and the broader organizational system of which they are a part. Cognitive systems (organizations) consist of leaders and key contributors who actively observe and monitor "the flow of their activities and expect others to do the same for their own; they also routinely monitor aspects, social and physical, of the contexts in which they move."[15]

---

* The OGI and this book are based on my research which are found in my doctoral thesis: "Innovative organizations as capable cognitive systems: Development and validation of the innovation quotient inventory."

At the same time, it is surmised that there is an underlying "cognitive architecture" operating within all organizations as cognitive systems that influence the thinking, actions, and decisions of the leaders and key contributors within it.

> *"The cognitive architecture, unique to each organization, influences — if not biases —*
> *its process of cognition: a recursive process of observation, reflection, and intended action. In other words, the cognitive architecture influences the way the organization seeks to achieve intelligent action."*

Organizations, as cognitive systems, possess a unique cognitive architecture, which is expressed through its cognitive, or archic style.

Furthermore, the cognitive architecture may serve to legitimize or de-legitimize the cognitive preferences, values, and beliefs of the individuals — themselves cognitive agents — comprising the cognitive system.

While organizational members ultimately take actions on behalf of their organizations, the implicit cognitive architecture, which impresses itself on those members within the cognitive system, may shape their actions *as if* it is an independently constituted, cognitive, and willful entity. You're probably aware of the catch in all of this.

There appears to exist a schism within cognitive systems, a duality between the cognitive competence of its members, and the cognitive architecture of the organization. Once we moved from the agrarian era into the industrial revolution and then on to the technological period, this duality has slowly grown as employees and organizations diverged in their needs, wants, agendas, and sense of purpose. The result is what we see today in business: a disparity between an organization's members and the organization perceived as an independent entity. Though organizations generally have a stated mission, vision and purpose, these may actually be at odds with what members perceive and desire to act upon.

The cognitive architecture within organizations is both the "medium and outcome" of the cognitive styles and practices that are recursively performed by members within the organizational system — though the members within those organizations aren't necessarily vested in those cognitive styles and practices. What is created is what's commonly referred to as "corporate culture."

The culture or environment of an organization — and the competing mindsets and agendas that cause organizations to falter — is what the OGI addresses. It measures organizational and employee mindsets, capturing the crucial emotional, intellective, and volitional elements that other diagnostic tools overlook. What is generated is a holistic organizational assessment.

That sounds rather simplistic, and enters territory that most organizations either prefer to avoid or to let HR handle. The old adage "the business of business is business" has held sway for far too long. People — the reason any organization exists — now want a voice in how they're treated and how they're incorporated into the organization as a whole. We're moving out of the "us vs. them" mentality — employees vs. management — and into the culture of "us" as producers, innovators, and winners.

To attain that position, a new definition of what it means to win and be a winner needs some discussion.

Chapter 1 References

1. James, Randy, "Jim Collins: How Mighty Companies Fall," Wednesday, *TIME Magazine*. June 10, 2009. http://content.time.com/time/business/article/0,8599,1903713,00.html

2. *Globe and Mail*, January 30, 2012.

3. Christensen, Clayton. *The Innovator's Dilemma: When New Technologies Cause Great Firms to Fail*, 2000. Introduction: xvi.

4. *Forbes*, February 4, 2014.

5. Lewin, Kurt. *Field Theory in Social Science*. Harper & Brothers Publishers, 1951: 169.

6. "Leadership and Innovation," *The McKinsey Quarterly*, 2008.

7. Goldin, Ian, and Chris Kutarna. *Age of Discovery*, 2016: 2.

8. Salk, Jonas and Jonathon Salk. *World Population and Human Values*, 1981: 94.

9. Emery, Fred E., and E.L Trist. *Towards a Social Ecology*. New York, NY: Plenum/Rosette Edition, 1973: 43.

10. Goldstein, Jeffrey, James K. Hazy, and Benyamin B. Lichtenstein. *Complexity and the Nexus of Leadership*. New York, NY: Palgrave Macmillan, 2010: 3.

11. Wagner, Carolyn S. *The New Invisible College: Science for Development*. Washington, DC: Brookings Institute Press, 2008: 34.

12. Ackoff, Russell L. *Ackoff's Best: His Classic Writings on Management*. 1st ed. New York, NY: John Wiley & Sons, 1999: 54.

13. Glynn, Mary Ann. "Innovative genius: A framework for relating individual and organizational intelligences to innovation." *Academy of Management Review.*, 1996

14. Maturana, Humberto. "Biology of cognition." Biological Computer Laboratory Research Report BCL 9.0: University of Illinois, 1970. Retrieved from http://biolinguagem.com/biolinguagem_anthropolgia/maturana_1970_biologyofcognition.pdf21(4): 4.

15. Giddens, Anthony. *The Constitution of Society*. Berkeley, CA: University of California Press, 1984: 5.

CHAPTER 2

WINNING *IS* EVERYTHING

*"In this world of hyper-accelerated change,
it seems all organizations are fighting for survival
whether it's for profits or for funding."*

In business, winning is connected with survival and is certainly critical to success, but it doesn't necessarily mean being first or top dog. Winning could mean satisfying shareholders; delighting customers, consumers, patients, or constituents; expanding market share; becoming more efficient or increasing profitability. What if we replaced the term "winning" with surviving or adapting? If we view winning from these perspectives, then, indeed, winning *is* everything for organizations.

What it means to win and the way success is measured depends on the type of organization and the context in which it functions. For example:

- In the commercial sector, winning means achieving or exceeding business and financial targets established by management at the beginning of each business cycle.

- In the education sector, success might mean enhancing the student experience or raising the academic credentials of the institution in order to attract higher calibre teachers and, of course, more students to their institutions who are, after all, their *raison d'être*.

- For non-profit organizations, success might mean finding alternative revenue sources to either sustain or expand their reach.

- For governments, success might mean more efficient, more convenient, or higher-value public services.
- In professional sports, winning or being first most often defines success.

Adapt or Die

Charles Darwin, the great Naturalist who developed the theory of natural selection, has typically been associated with the famous adage, "survival of the fittest," which implies life being a competitive battlefield in which only the strongest survive. In truth, he never actually phrased it quite that way, but he did say, "In the struggle for survival, the fittest win out at the expense of their rivals because they succeed in adapting themselves best to their environment," (from *On the Origin of Species*). In another related quote, Darwin said: "It's not the strongest of the species who survive, nor the most intelligent, but the one most responsive to change."

In other words, long-term survival requires an ability to interact with the ever-changing environment in cooperative, not just competitive, ways. It's not only brute strength nor is it just high intelligence, but an ability to shift thinking and behaviors in situationally adaptive ways to maintain survival within a context of change. Having said that, the ability to observe, assimilate and make adaptive shifts requires organizations to have a heightened level of cognitive competence to effectively address an increasingly complex business and global environment.

Cognitive Competence

Successful adaptation for organizations requires cognitive competence. Organizational systems must possess an inherent ability to absorb and respond to changes that occur within the environments in which they function. As such, organizations require an ability to effectively observe, ascribe meaning and respond to changes that occur both internally within their own systems and externally to the social, political, market, and/or competitive forces impacting their organization.

It is when organizations are out of "fit" with their environments that organizational decline can occur, threatening long-term survival. Being out of fit with the environment implies an inability to change in adaptive ways. The social systems law of *requisite variety*,[16] for example, suggests that an organization's internal environment must keep pace with the complexity of its external environment if it is to remain vital and survive over the long term. Cognitive competence requires an ability for leaders and key contributors within the organization to think systemically — embracing the nuances and complexities associated with growing interdependencies between people, systems, and processes — if they are to keep step with the increasingly complex environments in which they operate.

To clarify, when referring to systems or environments as "complex" to a greater or lesser degree, it represents a function of the number and variety of elements within a system and, importantly, the number of interactions and interdependencies that exist between those elements within the system.

Two important dimensions associated with cognitive competence that allow organizations to thrive in more complex environments include: *differentiation* and *integration*. Leaders who are able to differentiate and perceive multiple dimensions or characteristics in a situation or challenge — while also seeing the explicit and implicit interrelationships that exist between those elements — will likely make better decisions for their organizations operating in complex environments than those who are less able or unwilling to engage in systems-based thinking,[17]

Another related concept associated with cognitive competence speaks to the *absorptive capacity*[18] of organizations. Essentially, an organization's ability to learn and innovate is influenced by its ability to integrate, "absorb," and exploit external knowledge to enhance its adaptive efforts. For this to occur, organizations must a) be open and receptive to new information, b) be savvy enough to recognize their limitations so as to leverage new information or ideas that can augment their current stalk of knowledge, and c) be capable of responding with intelligent action.

Organizations must possess the ability to see beyond the horizon and attune themselves to disruptive signs, disconfirming evidence, and signals of significance. Otherwise, long-term survival is compromised. Unfortunately, when people and organizations feel under threat, they can become rigid or inflexible,[19] which only aggravates, if not, accelerates their demise.

Cognitive Incompetence Leads to Decline

It has been well documented that all organizations go through various stages or cycles starting with an initiation or birth phase, then on to a growth phase, followed by a maturity phase, and eventually decline if adaptive efforts through innovation and renewal are unsuccessful.[20] Organizations may also go through various stages of decline, which Chuck Williams described as: *blinded, inaction, faulty action, crisis, and dissolution*.[21]

The seeds of decline are often sown with a lack of organizational attention or sensitivity such that leaders are literally *blind* to potentially significant changes occurring in their environments. It's very difficult to act on things that fall outside of our awareness. And yet in the *inaction* stage, leaders do begin to "see" performance problems, but intentionally choose not to act on them. Cognitive blinders are perhaps at play here where leaders are looking for confirming evidence that supports the merits of past assumptions and ways of working that have led to success up to this point, thereby minimizing the significance of the problems they see occurring.

In the *faulty action* stage, organizations typically look for the band aid or quick fix solutions and choose not to address the deeper, more systemic causes that are damaging profits, market share, and/or customer value. For example, they may look for efficiencies, lay off workers, and cut costs for short-term wins while ultimately expecting the existing business model to eventually kick back into gear and return the company to previous levels of growth and profitability.

The *crisis* stage hits as a result of failing to sufficiently shift the organization's mindset and culture, which, ultimately, is required to change systems, processes, structures, and business models in adaptive ways. This aligns with the behavioural signs of organizational decline identified by Mische:[22]

10 Behaviours that Signal Decline

1. The organization exhibits a lack of understanding concerning the environmental and economic realities confronting it, or is in denial.

2. The management of the organization is arrogant with regard to its view of the world and assessment of its internal competencies. Example: Icarus Paradox*.

---

* See for example, Danny Miller's, *The Icarus Paradox: How Exceptional Companies Bring About Their Own Downfall*

3. The organization has lost perspective with respect to customers, products, suppliers, and competitors.
4. Management and employees have an insular focus or preoccupation with internal processes, internal measurements, and politics.
5. The organization has lost its sense of urgency and lacks an attitude of self-determination.
6. The organization is relying on historical and poorly conceptualized or inappropriate business strategies and traditional management methods to address new and different challenges.
7. The organization has the propensity to repeat mistakes and fails to learn from past experiences.
8. The organization has low or slow innovation practices and is late to market with new products/services.
9. The organization has a tendency to recycle marginally performing managers.
10. The organization relies exclusively on internal talent as a source of leadership.

Intelligent Action

When organizations hit the *crisis* stage, it is a clear indication that the system has not achieved *intelligent action*. All organizations are purposeful, willful entities capable of changing goals, systems, people, and even their structures to achieve more effective results.[23] Organizations, as cognitive systems, strive for intelligent action, meaning they are "intelligent" to the extent that they are able to act with relevance to sustain themselves.[24]

> *"Intelligent action describes the organization's ability to act in adaptive ways, remaining vital through change, as it strives to achieve its purpose and strategic vision …and live to fight another day."*

When in the *crisis* stage, organizations are, as the term indicates, in a state of high disruption with drastic measures being taken to save the company from complete dissolution.

- BlackBerry, formerly Research In Motion (RIM), provides a recent example of an organization that has moved through the various stages of decline and that has been in *crisis*, battling for survival, for several years. It has significantly restructured to focus on a core capability that will hopefully prevent complete *dissolution* of the company. In fact, it may be in a position to rise out of the ashes of decline, renewed and positioned for another cycle of accelerated growth with its sole focus now on software and licensing rather than the hardware (smartphone) market in which they once dominated.

- McDonald's is another example of company reeling from declining profits and striving to adapt to changing consumer values and "tastes" related to nutrition and health. It remains to be seen how they fair.

- Clothing apparel and financial sectors are currently in disruption facing heightened competition and shifting consumer mindsets that are increasingly accustomed to fast, easy-to-use e-based platforms to do their banking and to buy their clothes. For example, according to a 2016 Boston Consulting Group report titled, "Retail Bank Operational and Digital Leaders Reap the Rewards," banks that want to win in the new e-based, interconnected retail world will need to accelerate their digital transformation efforts.

They indicate that "banks leading in measures of operational and digital excellence [such as consumer and sales excellence, streamlined organization, and efficient processes] reaped the lion's share of financial rewards. They achieved 50% higher average pre-tax profit per customer than the median, while their operating expenses per customer were 30% less." [25]

The same could easily be said for any number of industries including traditional brick and mortar clothiers such as Tip Top Tailors owned by Grafton-Fraser, Inc. (which is now in dissolution), Moore's, Aeropostle, Abercrombie & Fitch, American Eagle Outfitters, and many others are struggling for survival in the shifting retail landscape.

In short, many organizations around the world are fighting for survival. In fact, 98 percent of American companies disappear within eleven years.[26] One CEO client of a multimillion-dollar organization I've worked with stated that his organization was "quietly fighting for survival." In his case, "winning" meant successfully balancing the needs of the board, government, and union with a new funding model required for the organization to remain viable in the future.

Another client, the CEO of a multibillion-dollar organization, indicated to me that "the top and the bottom of the organization are OK, it's the mushy middle" that they needed to address if they were to successfully transform their organization fast enough to meet current and emerging competitive pressures. Winning implied getting managers to think differently, to effectively change the organization's status quo in order to make them more efficient while successfully differentiating themselves from competitors and bringing new value to their customers.

This CEO's challenge could well be the mantra for the majority of organizations around the world in today's highly competitive, global market: *"be efficient, be unique, be innovative, and be quick."*

Winning and Surviving

If winning and being successful are conditional, then what are the factors that relate directly to business and its ability to more than just survive?

Innovation is definitively linked to organizational and national survival. In their book, *Innovation Economics*, Robert Atkinson and Stephen Ezell, contend that prior to 1995 "failure to innovate usually just meant slower growth… but today, the failure to innovate, particularly for developed nations, leads to failed companies, loss of export competitiveness, and ultimately structural economic crisis."

In "The Global CEO Study" conducted by IBM in 2006, drawing from 765 CEOs from around the world, it was reported that "globalization and technology are lifting competition to new heights…growth — perhaps even survival — depends on innovation."

In *The Rise of the Network Society*, Manuel Castells contends that "successful organizations are those able to generate knowledge and process information efficiently...and to innovate, as innovation becomes the key competitive weapon."

So, *innovation* is the new crucial mechanism in the process of transformation, thriving, and "winning." And one of the primary catalysts of innovation comes by way of technology, which is in fact creating disruption throughout most industries around the world.

- "In 2010 the US manufactured value added was 235% of 1970 levels — and was brought about with 33% less labour, which represents an extraordinary increase in productivity," brought about largely through technological innovation.[27]

- "Bank of America Merrill Lynch predicted that by 2025 the 'annual creative disruption impact' from AI (Artificial Intelligence) could amount to $14 trillion – $33 trillion, including a $9 trillion reduction in employment costs thanks to AI-enabled automation of knowledge work...."[28]

- Eighteen to twenty years out, technological advancements will be hundreds of thousands to a million times more advanced. In thirty years' time, bio, nano, robotic, and computer technology will become so rapid, so advanced, and so profound that today's limited understanding does not allow us to describe, within reason, what life will be like.[29]

- A substantial share of employment in service occupations are highly susceptible to computerization, as well as in manufacturing, clerical, retail, law, financial services, education, and medicine.[30]

- While GDP has risen, median income has not, and inequality has grown.[31]

In our relatively new network society, the internal and external demand for technological innovation within the digital frontier is without question a key culprit driving the need for organizations to innovate for survival. There continues to be a widening "disparity in profits between leading firms in industries that use technology intensively...[the] innovation laggards pay a stiff price, and sometimes the ultimate one: bankruptcy and dissolution," writes Robert Atkinson in his book, *Innovation Economics*.

Further, technological innovation in this century is occurring faster than we've ever experienced before in history. Erik Brynjolfsson and Andrew McAfee, in their book, *Race Against the Machine*, indicate that "already computers are thousands of times more powerful than they were 30 years ago, and all evidence suggests this pace will continue for at least another decade, and probably more."

Suffice it to say that computer technology is here to stay. Innovation in this arena doesn't look as if it's going to abate either.

Within the context of rapid technological and global change, no organization can afford to be resting on its heels. Innovation represents a core organizational capability needed to ensure long-term health and survival, and yet so many organizations, despite their best intentions, fail to get it right because they often underestimate the extent to which their organization's internal environment consisting of climate, culture, and mindsets influence their organization's ability to grow through new value creation and adaptive change.

Given the importance of innovation and successful transformation, what can organizations do to improve these important activities? Organizations as cognitive systems, do have an inherent ability to adapt and survive and return back to growth even after experiencing serious periods of decline (think of Apple and IBM). If winning and being successful are conditional, then what are the factors that relate directly to business and their ability to more than just survive?

The search for useful answers, I suggest, is best initiated with knowing how to frame the question. In other words, our approach to understanding innovation matters. Part of the challenge for some leaders may be that they attempt to isolate the activity of innovation from the organizational context in which it occurs. I believe this to be a critical error at the root of why many innovation efforts produce unsatisfactory results. Knowing where the seeds of successful innovation are sown within organizations is just as important as knowing what innovation is. We cannot truly understand one without the other and yet this logic appears to be counter-intuitive to many innovation efforts within organizations.

Inconvenient Truth #4
The goals of organizations and the goals of innovation are most often the same and yet the two are experienced by organizational members as enemies, not allies.

In my research over the last seven years, drawing from business and academic literature, as well as over twenty years' experience working as an organizational development consultant with organizations globally, I have found a number of Inconvenient Truths about innovation within organizations:

1. Leaders of organizations need better ways to measure, quantify, and demystify innovation so that it can be tangibly addressed in a systematic way.

2. Innovation is a leading indicator of an organization's ability to sustain future success.

3. The majority of organizations still view innovation as a "nice to have" not a "need to have," and they eventually pay the price. Those that do value and see the need for innovation struggle with how to do it well, or better.

4. The goals of organizations and the goals of innovation are most often the same and yet the two are experienced by organizational members as enemies, not allies.

5. Creativity is absolutely essential, but it's not the whole story.

6. An inability to break the bonds of short-term thinking at the leadership level will kill innovation.

7. Organizations are most often adept at short-term, incremental innovation, but are typically much less effective at long-term, transformative, or radical forms of innovation.

8. Failing to understand the full ramifications of the fact that organizations are complex systems, rather than a collection of complicated processes, will severely constrain an organization's transformational potential — their ability to initiate and sustain innovation.

9. There is no innovation without leadership support.

10. There is a dramatic need to better understand the relationship between organizational thinking and organizational innovation.

11. Effective organizations are most likely to be successful with innovation and yet it's the ineffective organizations that need it most and who often experience numerous failed innovation attempts, a.k.a. the vicious cycle.

12. Engagement surveys are useful, but not substantive enough to fully grasp, describe, and enable how to improve organizational innovation and transformation.

13. Innovation and transformation are every bit as emotional as intellectual for every member of an organization.*

These Inconvenient Truths about innovation may be new to you or you may already be familiar with some or all of them. Taken as a whole, they provide a framework from which you can base your own experiences with innovation, past, present, and future. As we progress through a high-level explanation of the OGI in this book, we'll refer back to specific ones as a refresher, but to also help you anchor to them. As Bob Iger, Chairman and CEO of the Walt Disney Company, said, "The heart and soul of the company is creativity and innovation."

Expanding the View of Innovation

Innovation is consistently described in literature as the creation and implementation of something new.[32] Importantly, "new" does not just mean new to the world, nor is it restricted to products. Innovation may also involve meaningful improvements or re-combinations of what already exists and may focus on products, processes, or services offered by an organization.[33]

Viewing innovation in this light, we can see that innovation is not restricted to commercially focused or profit-driven enterprises. It is equally important in the government, non-profit, health, and education sectors. In my research and practice, I define innovation as:

---

* I'm sure there are many more not listed here that you have found to be true in your own experience. Please add to the list at www.TheOGI.com.

> An organization's ability to stimulate and transform new ideas and knowledge into products, processes or services that tangibly increase value to customers, accelerate growth, enhance operational effectiveness, and/or improve profitability.

In this regard, innovation ought to be viewed as being woven into the fabric of organizational life and is in fact the life-blood of current and future success. Success is, of course, dependent on the organization's mission and purpose.

For instance, success in health care will most certainly include the effective treatment and care of patients. Innovation in this sector may focus on enhancing the quality of care that increases value to their patients. Enhanced value to their patients may include the development of new or improved processes and/or services, but likely would not typically include the development of new medical products or devices, *per se*, which is usually left to external, commercially focused medical system providers such as Siemens, Philips, and General Electric.

Success in the private sector, particularly publicly traded companies, typically includes increasing shareholder value through improved profitability. Innovations focused on continuous improvement and enhancing operational effectiveness such as through Lean or Six Sigma methodologies support greater operational efficiencies and help to drive down costs and eliminate wasteful activities throughout the value chain.

On the other hand, new product innovation within the private sector helps to drive organizational success through increased value to customers and accelerated growth, which is necessary for organizations to remain vital over the long term.

Business model innovation defined as "innovation in the structure and/or financial model of the business"[34] is becoming increasingly important for organizations as they continue to cope with technological innovation and accelerated competition "which has more than doubled in the past 40 years."[35]

Business model innovation may include various combinations of processes, services, or even product innovations. You may remember Dell Computers in the 1990s disrupting the personal computer industry by eliminating the retailer in the value chain, and thereby altering the financial model within the personal computer business.

More recently, think of the major banking institutions and automakers that are currently (or ought to be) racing to create new business models in order to compete with serious disruptors like Apple and Google: flush with cash and not only *quickly* becoming viable financial institutions, but automobile makers as well.

Over the years, a number of insights emerged as I worked with leaders and key contributors with an array of sectors including, manufacturing, consumer packaged goods, education, and health care. What we ascertained is that, collectively, groups within all organizations associated innovation with:

- creative new ideas
- creating something new
- thinking outside-the-box
- breaking out of long-established patterns
- new ways of looking at things
- making things better, different

No doubt the notion of "creativity" certainly stands out and is typically at the forefront in the minds of most leaders when asked about organizational innovation. The need for creativity cannot be underestimated. New thinking and fresh ideas are the fuel of innovation and change. Great! But, at the same time, however, like the cars we drive, it takes more than fuel to turn the wheels of innovation effectively — and in the right direction. It's akin to knowing how to drive correctly when skidding on ice.

Inconvenient Truth #5
Creativity is absolutely essential, but it's not the whole story.

Deeper discussions with leaders bring forth interesting perspectives that highlight pervasive aspects of organizational innovation beyond the presence or need for "creativity." Specifically, the way leaders and key contributors actually *experience* innovation within their organizations tells a deeper tale related to the factors that influence an organization's ability to innovate effectively.

Innovation involves change and there's no way of avoiding, deferring, camouflaging, or denying it. It requires people to shift the way they think about themselves, their functions, their processes and habits, and their organizations. Argh!

Change — challenges to our conventional ways of thinking and doing — can generate an array of emotional reactions such as fear, excitement, frustration, anger, or even relief for those who have been waiting a long time for or dreading what they deem to be needed change.

"The connection between innovation and change cannot be lost. Change is part of the context in which innovation occurs and evolves."

In most organizations, too much change too fast creates confusion and an environment for error and distrust, which is not a good outcome, particularly, for example, in healthcare organizations where patient safety is paramount. Effective change management and sustainability are required. A sensitivity to the culture of the organization is important, as well as maintaining a sense of timing and pacing for introducing innovation into the organization. For example, as depicted in Figure 1, if there is too little innovation, organizational effectiveness is diminished, but as innovation is stepped up and integrated, so will effectiveness likely improve.

Figure 1. Organizational Effectiveness vs. Innovation/Change Introductions

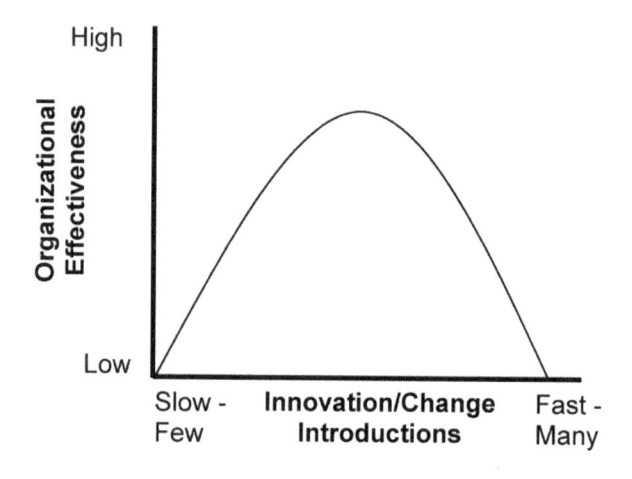

Conversely, too much innovation too fast will likely decrease organizational effectiveness. The introduction of any innovation(s) is a studied process, one that the OGI makes readily visible. Once an assessment is completed, that's when leadership steps in to spearhead implementation and all that that entails.

Effective Leadership and Innovation

The presence of effective leadership is a key determinant in an organization's ability to innovate well. Senior leaders and innovation leaders must be mindful of the way in which innovation impacts an organization, as well as how the organizational system as a whole impacts any innovation(s). Consistency and persistence in staying attuned to the organization's capacity for innovation at any given time is critical.

- Leaders need to maintain a healthy tension between the change effects brought about by innovation across the organization.

- The anticipated positive impact intended to ultimately improve organizational effectiveness and long-term success must also be factored in.

It's easy to recognise that there is positive energy associated with an organization that is innovative and that helps to drive and empower effectiveness. It can remain a virtuous cycle as long as the leadership and entire team ensures any innovation(s) positively contributes to organizational effectiveness from top to bottom.

Leaders need to be instrumental in developing strategic linkages to innovation, selecting the right kinds of innovations to optimize organizational effectiveness, and introduce those innovations appropriately and within the context of other change efforts that may be occurring within the organizational ecosystem.

Figure 2. The Ecosystem of Organizational Innovation

Labels around central "Organizational Innovation": Customers, Information Technology (IT), Senior Leadership, Production, Government, Universities, Finance, Marketing, Operations, Legal/Regulatory Affairs, Engineering, R&D, Venture Capital, Innovation Teams, Sales, Partners

Essentially, effective organizations help to mitigate feelings of risk for all the organizational members. When individuals are innovating in a well-functioning organization, it makes it safer to continue to innovate, people have a voice, they are encouraged to engage and contribute, and that is what helps to develop an effective organization.

As just mentioned, the flip side of positive innovation is "risk." Risk is often and aptly focused on the outcomes of innovation and yet it is apparent that the *affective* or *emotional* tone within the organizational environment influences the willingness of members to withstand the professional, if not personal, risks associated with leading or supporting an innovation that may ultimately fail, or be shelved. For example, managers in one large organization I've worked with voiced frustration from the standpoint that it was difficult for teams to get excited about innovation projects because so often they lost momentum due to shifting organizational priorities. Given this happened often, it was tough to get excited and committed to the next innovation project. The added challenge was that organizational members felt compelled to participate, perceiving "career limiting" risks associated with not getting involved in yet another potentially empty shell innovation project disseminated from senior leaders. Inconvenient Truth #6 was alive and well in this organization given the leadership's chronic focus on short-term results which sucked resources away from innovation projects.

Inconvenient Truth #6
An inability to break the bonds of short-term thinking at the leadership level will kill innovation.

Challenging the prevailing mindsets within the organization is indeed risky. As many leaders indicated in my research, "…it's a gamble, taking the chance, when not knowing how your new ideas will be received."

If we view innovation as a *whole system* phenomenon, it can dramatically change a Top Team's approach to improving their organization's innovative capability and capacity. Innovation activities can either be internally focused on process improvements geared to improving productivity or service delivery, or externally focused activities designed to support growth through the creation and development of new products, new markets, and new customers.

Inconvenient Truth #7
Organizations are most often adept at short-term, incremental innovation, but are typically much less effective at long-term, transformative, or radical forms of innovation.

It can be argued that most organizations are more adept at internally focused innovation given that it is more tangible and more closely aligned to the operational mindset that pervades most organizations.

Externally focused innovation is generally more of a challenge for organizations. Creating and developing new products for growth and "exploration" typically stretch the organization's mindset beyond their comfort zone of short-term, operational thinking and controls.

Organizations tend to be better at optimizing or exploiting existing products and resources and less effective at developing new products and services that require alternative resources to reach new markets and customers. The crux is that innovation is a process woven into the fabric of every organization, whether it is explicit or not and whether desired or not.

Inconvenient Truth #8
*Failing to understand the full ramifications
of the fact that organizations are complex systems,
rather than a collection of complicated processes,
will severely constrain an organization's transformational
potential — their ability to initiate and sustain innovation.*

That brings us back to this chapter's title: "Winning *is* Everything." The concept of winning involves more than just beating out the competition. Today, winning requires a change in mindset, one that fully integrates innovation and creativity into the very fabric of an organization. No matter the kind of organization or what its unique purpose may be, innovation represents an essential capability and capacity needed to ensure sustained success, viability, and survival.

And "mindset"? It's the magic word upon which the alchemy of the OGI is grounded. Without a shift in mindset, it's impossible to move in any direction, impossible to be creative — impossible to drive growth, innovation, and positive transformation.

Chapter 2 References

16. Ashby, Ross W. *Introduction to Cybernetics*, Chapman & Hall: London, 1956.
17. Jean Bartunek, Judith Gordon and Rita Weathersby. "Developing Complicated Understanding in Administrators," *The Academy of Management Review* 1983. See also Streufert and Swezey, *Complexity, Managers and Organizations*, Academic Press, 1986.
18. Wesley, Cohen and Daniel Levinthal. "Absorptive Capacity: A New Perspective on Learning and Innovation," *Administrative Science Quarterly*, 1990.
19. Barrett, Carole and Michael Pratt, "From Threat-Rigidity to Flexibility," *Journal of Organizational Change Management*, 2000.
20. Quinn, Robert E., and Kim S. Cameron, "Organizational Life Cycles and Shifting Criteria of Effectiveness," *Management Science*, 1983.
21. Williams, Chuck, *MGMT: Principles of Management*. 8th ed. South-western Pub., 2015.
22. Mische, Michael A. *Strategic Renewal: Becoming a High-Performance Organization*. 1st ed. Upper Saddle River, NJ: Prentice Hall, 2000: 25-30.
23. Ackoff, Russell L. *Ackoff's Best: His Classic Writings on Management*. 1st ed. New York, NY: Wiley, 1999.
24. Maturana, Humberto. *Biology of Cognition*, Biological Computer Laboratory Research Report BCL 9.0, 1970.
25. www.bcgperspectives.com/content/articles/financial-institutions-technology-digital-retail-bank-operational-digital-leaders-reap-rewards/
26. Carlson, Curtis and William Wilmot. *Innovation: The Five Disciplines for Creating What Customers Want*, New York: Crown Business, 2006: 34-35.
27. *The US Manufacturing Renaissance: How Shifting Global Economics Are Creating an American Comeback*, The Boston Consulting Group, Inc., 2012.
28. *The Economist*, June 25, 2016.
29. http://theemergingfuture.com/speed-technological-advancement.htm
30. www.news.com.au/technology/science/robots-to-replace-almost-50-per-cent-of-the-work-force/story-fn5fsgyc-1226729696075
31. www.technologyreview.com/s/515926/how-technology-is-destroying-jobs/
32. Van de Ven & Poole, 1980; Schumpeter, 1983; Amabile, 1996a, 1996b.
33. Breznitz & Murphree, 2011.
34. The Global CEO Study, "Expanding the Innovation Horizon," 2006, IBM Global Services, p. 11.
35. Hagel III, John, John Seely Brown and Lang Davison, "The Big Shift," *Harvard Business Review*, July-August 2009.

CHAPTER 3

MINDSETS MATTER

*"A mindset represents more than how we think —
it captures how we feel and how we act within the world."*

We all possess a mindset. Our mindsets represent and impart a way of experiencing the world. We may think of a mindset as a lens through which we interpret and make meaning of the world around us. In fact, mindsets help to characterize who we are as individuals because they draw upon underlying values, beliefs, emotions, experiences, and thinking preferences that influence how we engage with the world around us.

As such, it is helpful to understand the mindsets of individuals and indeed whole organizations because they influence how people and organizations make meaning of, and subsequently respond to, the situations and challenges they face, as well as innovate and adapt.

Appreciating the full force of a mindset requires an understanding of the elements within our minds that contribute to its pervasive power to influence our lives.

Mindsets Influence Our Actions

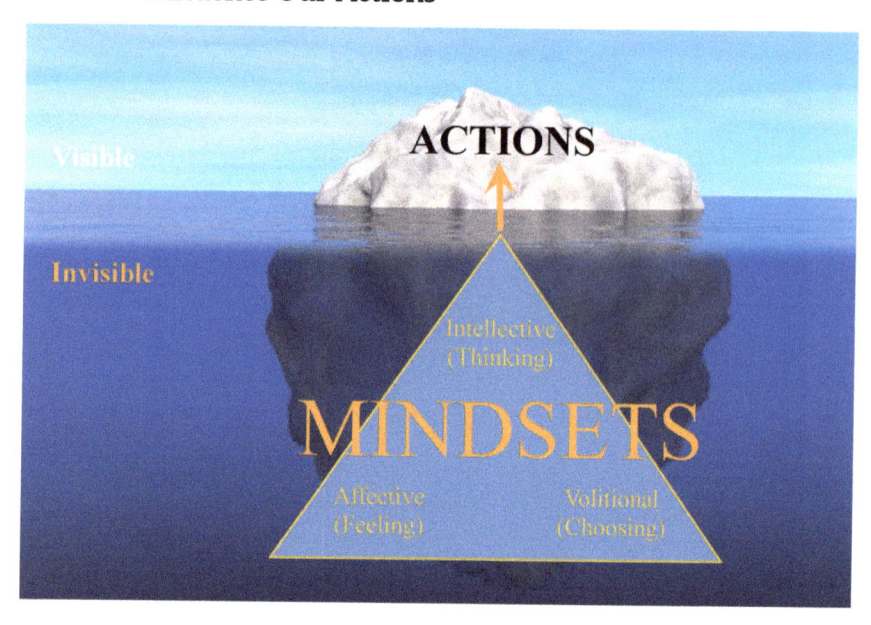

Visible: ACTIONS

Invisible: MINDSETS
- Intellective (Thinking)
- Affective (Feeling)
- Volitional (Choosing)

A mindset is not just about how we think in the traditional sense, but also involves emotional and motivational predispositions that collectively influence our actions. Equally important, our mindsets usually operate below the level of our awareness and are not fully appreciated unless we focus our attention on them, or we are confronted with a situation that brings forth underlying elements of our mindsets into conscious awareness.

From a practical standpoint, a "mindset" is descriptive of how our minds work in action. For example, think about your political orientation. This can be a helpful representation of mindsets in action. How do you feel about your political party? How do you feel about the others? When listening to your candidate, do you resonate with their perspective on the world? Do you feel a willingness to follow them and support them?

Our particular political mindset influences not only how we think about those involved, but also how we feel and respond to those we support and those we don't.

The fundamental elements of mindsets are:

- Affective (Feeling) — "I believe you and feel connected to you."

- Intellective (Thinking) — "I see and understand your point of view."
- Volitional (Choosing) — "I choose to support you and will vote for you."

Now try to remove any of these three dimensions from your own political orientation. It's very difficult to do, as they are so intertwined with one another, each influencing and connecting with the other two. How I feel about something or someone very much influences how I think about them or it, and in turn influences the way I will respond to the person or situation at hand.

Mindsets Are Both Mirrors and Windows

Carol Dweck, a professor of psychology at Stanford University, has advanced the distinction between "fixed" and "growth" mindsets primarily related to people's perceived views concerning their abilities.[36] As "mirrors," mindsets are fundamentally a reflection of what we believe about ourselves.

- For those who hold a "fixed" mindset, their talents, abilities, and intelligence are typically perceived as in-born — you either have them or you don't.
- Those with a "growth" mindset maintain a view that their own capabilities can be improved with focused effort and dedication.

Dweck's insightful work aligns with other prominent researchers, such as Howard Gardner, David Perkins and Robert Sternberg who all challenge the thinking that intelligence is "fixed," particularly as it has been traditionally assessed by way of the IQ (Intelligence Quotient). These researchers contend that there are different types of intelligences — Logical, Visual, Musical, Intrapersonal, Kinesthetic, Interpersonal, Naturalistic, Linguistic — that are "learnable" and that individuals uniquely possess.

Mindsets, from Dweck's view, represent "self" concepts and beliefs, which may either be self-limiting or self-expanding. In my research, I've discerned that mindsets are not just about beliefs we hold about ourselves and our own personal capabilities. They are also reflective of how we view the world around us. In this regard, mindsets are also like windows in that they influence what we pay attention to in our external world.

Mindsets influence how we go about choosing what is important and meaningful in our daily lives. They influence how we interact with others, as well as how we go about problem solving, decision making, and adapting to situations and challenges we face at home and at work every day.

Dweck largely uses mindsets to describe core beliefs individuals possess centred around perceived capabilities related to learning and personal growth and development. The mindsets I've described in this book operate more like *world views* that shape the attention, selection, interpretation and utilization of facts, information, knowledge and values used by people, organizations, and whole societies as they seek to enact their worlds.

Mindsets Matter

Having introduced a basic concept of mindsets, let's identify the specific mindsets that all organizations possesses whether they are commercially focused, not-for-profit, governmental, health, or educationally focused.

> *"All organizational types demonstrate preferred mindsets, which influence the way they seek to fulfill their purpose and strategic mandate."*

As an organizational theorist and practitioner, I believed it was important to develop a valid, yet practical model and approach to identify the core mindsets at the root of adaptive action for all organizations. Of particular interest was understanding the mindsets that support an organization's ability to grow through innovation and adaptive change given the imperative for all organizations to find new ways to create value and remain relevant within a context of hyper-accelerated change.

If culture is an organization's personality, then mindset is its cognitive style

I originally labelled what are now called mindsets as "archic cognitive styles," which while technically accurate, was certainly quite a mouthful. The term "archic" simply implies primary, foundational, or first principle as in *architecture* or *archetype*. It has been well researched that we possess preferred cognitive (thinking) styles, which may be described as favoured ways in which we use the array of skills and abilities we possess. I propose that organizations also possess distinct cognitive stylistic preferences that until now have received far less attention.

Organizations also have preferred ways in which they utilize the skills, talents, and resources available within them in order to achieve their strategic and business objectives. But it goes even further than that and here's why:

"I contend that there are in fact 4 Principal Mindsets
upon which all organizations may either choose to adopt or avoid.
The extent to which each organization
utilizes these 4 Principal Mindsets in combination
is not only reflective of what the organization values,
but also points to its ability to achieve intelligent action."

From my research, mindsets can be explored at various levels of analysis: individual, group, and organizational. Actually, whole societies or nations may possess a dominant mindset. For example, in his book, *The Geography of Thought*,[37] Richard Nisbett describes extensive research that he and his colleagues have conducted exploring the differences in mindsets between Western and Eastern cultures. The table below identifies a few of the key distinctions identified in their research:

Differences in How Western and Eastern Cultures Think	
Western Culture	**Eastern Culture**
Analytical Thinking	Systems Thinking
Elements	Context
Logic	Inference
Objective	Subjective
Independence	Interdependence
Either/Or	Both/And
Categories	Relationships
Individual Action	Collective Action
Universal Rules Across Situations	Rules are Relative to Situation
Direct	Indirect
Objects – focusing on what it is, e.g., a statue	Substances – focusing on what it's made of e.g., a block of marble

As we can see, different cultures can possess very distinct mindsets which colour their worldviews, and so can organizations. At the organizational level of analysis, understanding an organization's mindset is critical given that it illuminates the underlying cognitive stylistic preferences that serve to direct the allocation of attention, energy, and resources deployed to support organizational success.

Making an organization's underlying mindset visible throughout the organization and with all stakeholders allows leaders to objectively assess the extent to which their current mindset is in line with where it needs to be in order to achieve sustained success amidst an ever-changing market and competitive environment.

The practical conversation between leaders within organizations related to mindsets may sound like this:

1. What is our organization's mindset?
2. How adaptive is our organization's current mindset?
3. To what extent do we need to shift our organization's mindset if we are to successfully grow or transform our culture, talent, systems, and processes to achieve our current and future strategic mandate?

Given that organizations need to think differently and challenge conventional practices, understanding an organization's current mindset serves as an important first step in generating adaptive changes in not only how the organization thinks, but how it *feels* and practically *responds* to the call for change, keeping in mind that…

> *"…a mindset represents more than how we think, it captures how we feel and how we act as individuals and as whole organizations."*

The 4 Principal Mindsets for Organizations

The following model demonstrates the 4 Principal Mindsets, which at their core may be understood as four fundamental ways of viewing the world. The anthropologist, David Dilworth, aptly suggests that "a worldview always puts forward a dominant sense of what is real, displacing or subordinating other forms of [knowing] to its own."[38] Each Mindset is in fact unique and valid in its own right offering a distinct cognitive frame that shapes the way in which the reality of lived experience is constructed and acted upon. Collectively, the 4 Principal Mindsets represent a holistic representation of the extraordinary variety of perspectives that truly enrich the tapestry of our human experience.

This model can be applied to a wide variety of contexts or overlaid onto numerous fields of study. The focus of this book relates to understanding the mindsets within organizations particularly as they relate to growth and adaptive change. These mindsets are in fact quantified within the OGI diagnostic and are connected, in the next chapter, to various organizational types and leadership styles. Each of them offers an important contribution to organizational life, and each are required to support growth and long-term success for organizations of any kind.

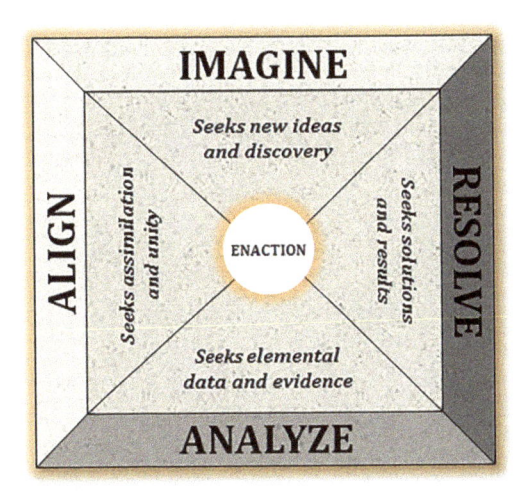

IMAGINE — *Seeks new ideas and discovery*
RESOLVE — *Seeks solutions and results*
ANALYZE — *Seeks elemental data and evidence*
ALIGN — *Seeks assimilation and unity*
ENACTION (center)

Enaction

In the center of the diagram, you'll see the word "enaction." Enaction refers to active engagement with the world. It suggests that we play an active role in the formulation of our given reality. We are not passive observers within the world. We are, in fact, active participants in how we experience — and indeed cognitively construct — the world in which we live.

The term "enaction" sits at the core of the model because we can choose to make meaning of, experience, and engage the world through the lens of four primary windows of reality. Enaction points to an expanded view of cognition — what I've termed "connective cognition" — given it integrates the mutually interdependent relationship that exists between how we think, feel, and act within the world.

Four Mindsets: "Windows on the World"

These 4 Principal Mindsets have been derived through a robust review of literatures from organizational psychology, sociology, philosophy, and anthropology. It appears that for millennia, the human psyche has been conceptualized as a quaternity, meaning it is composed of four primary parts.[39] Images of a circle divided into four parts can be dated as far back as the Stone Age as seen in Rhodesian rock drawings.[40] The renowned psychologist, Carl Jung, suggests "the quaternity is an organizing schema par excellence…it is a system of coordinates that is used almost instinctively for dividing up and arranging a chaotic multiplicity."[41]

Mandalas, often depicted as squares within a circle, are a good example of the universality of the quaternity image embedded within the human psyche.

Tibetan Mandala   Celtic Mandala

From the Native-American Medicine Wheel, Tibetan and Indonesian temples, to the gothic cathedrals in Europe, mandalas (squares within a circle and circles and labyrinths within circles) represent the quest for psychic harmony, wholeness, liberation, and development.[42] Examples of the quaternity utilized as an organizing framework to structure, if not simplify, the complexities of human experience are exhaustive, but here are just a few examples spanning various cultures, disciplines, and eras.

Source				
4 Personality Types[43]	Thinking	Feeling	Intuiting	Sensing
4 World Views[44]	Mechanism	Organicism	Contextualism	Formism
4 Drive Theory[45]	Learn	Bond	Acquire	Defend
4 Philosophic Types[46]	Democritean	Platonic	Sophistic	Aristotelean
4 Great Powers – The Medicine Wheel[47]	Wisdom (North)	Innocence (South)	Introspection (East)	Illumination (West)
4 Yogic Practices[48] or Spiritual Paths	Bhakti	Karma	Raja	Jnana

While a case could be made that there are other significant numbers, such as three (the Holy Trinity) or seven (days of the week), the quaternity is a dominant archetypal image that resides deep within the human psyche across multiple cultures.

Our ultimate goal as conscious, intentional human beings is not only to exist and sustain life, but to also make meaning of the world in which we live. We as human beings are meaning makers. The process in which we make meaning is intimately tied to the way in which we frame, perceive, and experience our world. The 4 Principal Mindsets represent fundamental ways of "knowing," which can be seen to influence the worldviews of scientists and philosophers across cultures and histories. In this book, we are zeroing in on how the 4 Principal Mindsets play an active role in supporting leaders and their organizations to both frame and advance their efforts to accelerate growth through innovation and adaptive change.

IMAGINE Motto: "Create the Future"

The ability of leaders, teams, and organizations to "imagine" is essential to innovation and adaptive change. Curiosity, a thirst for inspiration, and a belief in the power of possibility all fuel the search to discover something new. An ability to first imagine the future is essential to subsequently shaping it in a way that supports growth through innovative and adaptive change in order to achieve long-term success.

The worldview of imagine is such that it looks beyond conventional wisdom, advancing toward new forms of knowledge and challenging what we currently know or believe to be true. Organizations that epitomize the Imagine Mindset include: Cirque du Soleil, DreamWorks, and Pixar.

With the imagine Mindset, we are not fettered by attachments to norms, beliefs, or ways of working or living that may in any way constrain our ability to think anew. We are energized when solving problems by liberating ourselves and others from any attachments to rules, customs, knowledge, or traditions that may constrain our quest for the discovery of an effective outcome.

Organizations with an *IMAGINE* Mindset

Focus	New ideas and discovery.
Organizational Currency	New ideas are valued and rewarded.
Leadership	Leaders are visionary. They tend to put a lot of effort around developing an entrepreneurial, creative environment where employees are encouraged to take risks, challenge the status quo, and to think differently.
Risk	Lack of structure to optimize new ideas.
Reward	Remain relevant through proactivity, novelty, and a focus on creating new value for those you serve.

RESOLVE Motto: "Make it Work"

The ability to "resolve" internally and externally driven challenges along the innovation path is critical to transforming and adapting new ideas into tangible value for the organization. Individuals, teams, and whole organizations are compelled to find practical solutions to achieve value-added results.

The worldview of Resolve is such that knowledge and understanding are gained through practical experience and reflective inquiry surrounding those experiences. Organizations that epitomize the Resolve Mindset include: the World Bank, the International Monetary Fund (IMF) and the World Health Organization (WHO).

Viewing the world pragmatically allows for an objective approach that seeks to view concepts and challenges in relation to a wider context. We are energized when solving problems by connecting and integrating the parts of the challenge in relation to a wider context.

Organizations with a *RESOLVE* Mindset

Focus	Solutions and performance.
Organizational Currency	Results are valued and rewarded.
Leadership	Leaders are pragmatic. They tend to put a lot of effort around efficiently solving problems to ensure effective performance. Resolving external challenges to achieve results is essential.
Risk	Reactive approach. Chronic firefighting.
Reward	Fulfill commitments to customers and shareholders on time and on budget.

ANALYZE Motto: "Research Drives Knowledge"

The ability to "analyze" information, knowledge and ideas efficiently is a critical capability for effective innovation, transformation, and adaptability. An accurate appraisal of the internal and external environment drives a more practical and robust search for ideas and practices that will improve the status quo.

The worldview of Analyze is such that it seeks to build ideas, concepts, and theories from the ground up. The only way to really know something is to deconstruct it by breaking it down to its most fundamental or basic elements. Organizations that epitomize the Analyze Mindset include: the National Science Foundation (NSF), European Council for Nuclear Research (CERN) and the National Aeronautical Space Agency (NASA).

An objective, evidence-based approach to validating, understanding facts, and generating knowledge is considered paramount. We are energized when solving problems by breaking them down into their basic elements so as to pinpoint the essential aspects of the situation or challenge.

Organizations with an *ANALYZE* Mindset

Focus	Information and proof.
Organizational Currency	Facts and evidence are valued and rewarded.
Leadership	Leaders are analytical. They tend to put a lot of effort around developing systems and procedures to maximize a reliable search for knowledge, truth, and evidence to support the organization's strategic mandate.
Risk	Analysis paralysis. Stifling creativity and imagination.
Reward	Objective, evidence-based approach to the world.

ALIGN Motto: "Unity and Purpose"

The ability of leaders to "align" an organization's values and strategic vision with a transformation or innovation agenda is critical for organizational members to assimilate the purpose of change and thereby adapt. Given that people are the lifeblood of innovation, receptivity and emotional commitment are required to affect positive change through innovation.

The worldview of Align is such that knowledge and understanding are gained through conceptualizing the interrelationships between things. It attempts to assimilate facts, knowledge, and ideas into a comprehensive understanding of the whole picture. Organizations that epitomize the Align Mindset include: the United Nations (UN), the North Atlantic Treaty Organization (NATO), the World Heritage Fund, and all Labour Unions around the world.

Viewing the world systemically and revealing/discovering the interdependencies between things offers a robust, holistic appreciation and understanding of how things are. We are energized when solving problems by integrating and connecting aspects of the challenge with core values and a higher purpose.

Organizations with an *ALIGN* Mindset

Focus	Unity and integration.
Organizational Currency	Shared values and alignment of those values is encouraged and rewarded.
Leadership	Leaders are participative. They tend to put a lot of effort around developing a culture where employees feel emotionally connected and aligned to the organization, its vision, and purpose.
Risk	Too internally focused. Lacking competitive intensity.
Reward	Engaged, motivated, and aligned leadership team and workforce committed to fulfilling the organization's purpose.

As we've seen, the organization's dominant mindset plays an integral role in shaping how leaders approach innovation and change. To reiterate, organizational mindsets as defined and described in this book are not just indicative of how organizations think. Mindsets represent the preferred operational styles and procedures employed within the organization, which means they are also expressions of how things actually get done. The behaviours and actions of organizational members seeking to fulfill its mission, strategic priorities, and business goals are in fact demonstrations of the organization's mindset in action.

This is an important distinction. Case in point, a very good recent article titled, "10 Principals of Organization Culture,"[49] which has some terrific points related to culture change, describes mindsets in the traditional sense as "attitudes and beliefs that are widely shared, but exclusively invisible" while implying that mindsets are different from how people feel, their emotions, and how they behave.

The authors suggest that leaders ought to focus on "changing the most critical behaviours — the mindsets will follow." Simply "communicating values and putting them on glossy brochures" or "over-relying on top-down messaging" — activities associated with mindsets — will not be enough to change on organization's culture. This is absolutely true, but is not indicative of how mindsets are understood, and in fact measured and made visible within organizations as we'll see in the next chapter.

Chapter 3 References

36. Dweck, Carol. *Mindset: The New Psychology of Success*, New York, NY: Random House, 2006.
37. Nisbett, Richard. *The Geography of Thought: How Asians and Westerners Think Differently…and Why*, New York, NY: Free Press, 2003.
38. Dilworth, David. *Philosophy in World Perspective: A Comparative Hermeneutic of the Major Theories.* 1st ed. New Haven, CT: Yale University Press, 1989: 29.
39. Mitroff, Ian. *Stakeholders of the Organizational Mind: Toward a New View of Organizational Policy Making.* 1st ed. San Francisco, CA: Jossey-Bass, 1983.
40. Jung, C.G. *The Spirit in Man, Art and Literature*, Princeton, NJ: Princeton University Press, 1978.
41. Jung, C.G., and Gerhard Adler. *Aion: Researches into the Phenomenology of the Self.* Princeton, NJ: Princeton University Press, 1979: 242.
42. Fincher, Susanne. *Creating Mandalas: For Insight, Healing, and Self-Expression.* Boulder, CO: Shambala, 1991.
43. Storr, Anthony. *The Essential Jung: Essential Writings Introduced by Anthony Storr.* Princeton, NJ, Princeton University Press, 1994.
44. Pepper, Stephen C. *World Hypotheses: A Study in Evidence.* Oakland, CA: University of California Press, 1970.
45. Lawrence, Paul, and Nitin Nohria. *Driven: How Human Nature Shapes our Choices.* San Francisco, CA: Jossey-Bass, 2002.
46. Watson, Walter. *The Architectonics of Meaning: Foundations of the New Pluralism.* Chicago, IL: University of Chicago Press, 1993; see also David Dilworth, *Philosophy in World Perspective*, 1989.
47. Storm, Hyemeyohsts. *Seven Arrows.* New York, NY: Ballantine 1972. (Native American)
48. Smith, Huston. *The Religions of Man.* New York: Perennial Library, 1986. (Hinduism)
49. Katzenbach, John, Carolin Oelschlegel and James Thomas, "10 Principles of Organizational Culture," Strategy+Business, February 15, 2016.

CHAPTER 4

What's Your Organization's Mindset?

*"An organization's mindset is reflective
of the way it goes about the iterative process of
observation, reflection, decision making, and action."*

Understanding an organization's mindset is critical when it comes to growth and transformation because it encapsulates what the organization inherently values and what it chooses to pay attention to, both implicitly and explicitly.

What an organization selects as meaningful and important influences the kinds of judgments and decisions it makes, which in turn impacts the results it gets. For example, if its mindset is such that it believes driving efficiencies is the path to sustained success, it will focus on cost containment. Focusing on cost containment directs managerial attention to activities that will support those efforts.

This belief system reinforces and rewards shorter-term thinking, and limits activities and spending that do not seem to have a proven, justified, or quick ROI. Under this scenario, organizational attention and will is pulled away from growth-focused, innovative activities, so resources required for such activities are limited.

Case in point, the importance of organizational mindset is clearly witnessed in the "CEO Challenge 2015"[50] report produced by the Conference Board, which indicates the movement away from "cost-related defensive strategies such as reducing labour costs through staff reductions," which were understandably spurned on by the great recession. Now the trend is shifting toward "more growth-oriented, aggressive monetary and time-investment strategies in intangibles, such as business process redesign, improving workforce and leadership skills, and employee engagement and productivity." Clearly two different organizational mindsets at play, which have profound implications on what gets done and what gets rewarded, as well as varying workplace experience for leaders and key contributors within those organizations.

In Figure 3, we see a stylized version of the "iceberg model," which indicates that what we see on the surface is only a small fraction of what's true. In other words, there's far more than what meets the eye, particularly when it comes to understanding the actions of human and organizational systems. When leaders only focus on surface data (data that's readily available) to rationalize underperformance, they may miss the underlying, systemic root causes, which, if left unaddressed, will continue to constrain the organization's ability to grow and thrive successfully into the future.

Inconvenient Truth #9
There is no innovation without leadership support.

The results organizations get — the extent to which they realize their vision and business strategy — are largely influenced by the way they think, feel, and act. The word "act" rather than "do" or "behave" is used for a particular reason. The distinction between "action" versus "behaviour" is important and nicely distinguished by Jonathon Sacks.[51] He writes:

> "Behaviour is a physical movement, like raising a hand. An action is a movement with a purpose and intention. I can raise my hand to ask a question, hail a taxi, demonstrate support, or wave to a friend: same behaviour, different actions."

We can easily observe "What" people and organizations do — their visible behaviours in a rather detached, objective way. But to truly understand the actions that people and organizations take, we need to understand "Why" — the underlying motives, values, and intentions that are driving their unique actions. In other words, we need to understand *how* they think and feel.

Figure 3: The Iceberg Model

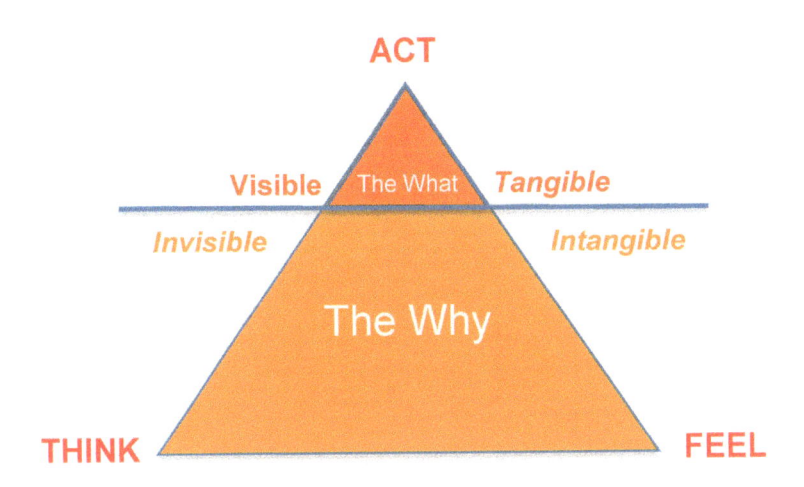

```
                    ACT
                     /\
                    /  \
          Visible / The  \ Tangible
         ─────── /  What  \ ───────
         Invisible         Intangible
               /            \
              /   The Why    \
             /                \
            /_____\
       THINK                    FEEL
```

Understanding Organizational Environments

Given that many leaders are now interested in gearing up their organizations for growth, efforts to improve performance must include a meaningful exploration of the working environment. While leaders have limited control over what happens in their *external* working environments, they have high degrees of control over and development of what happens within their organization's *internal* environment.

There are primarily three levels at which to view and understand an organization's environment: its climate, its culture and its mindset, as shown in the following Figure 4. The first two, climate and culture, are relatively well known, relevant and well researched. However, when it comes to understanding an organization's ability to grow and transform adaptively, understanding the organization's mindset is also critical, and here's why.

Organizations are cognitive systems striving to achieve intelligent action, meaning their intention is to make smart choices that will lead to organizational success. The organization's mindset is reflective of "The How" — the way it goes about the iterative process of observation, reflection, decision making, and action.

Importantly, mindset refers to the way an organization selects, interprets and makes use of the data and information it extracts from the environment and, therefore, influences the kinds of data it deems to be relevant and the kinds of strategies it ultimately selects to support organizational success. An organization's mindset is important because it influences the formulation of internal strategies, goals and objectives, as well as the way it perceives and reacts to external situations and occurrences happening within its broader market environment.

Figure 4: Elements of the Organization's Environment

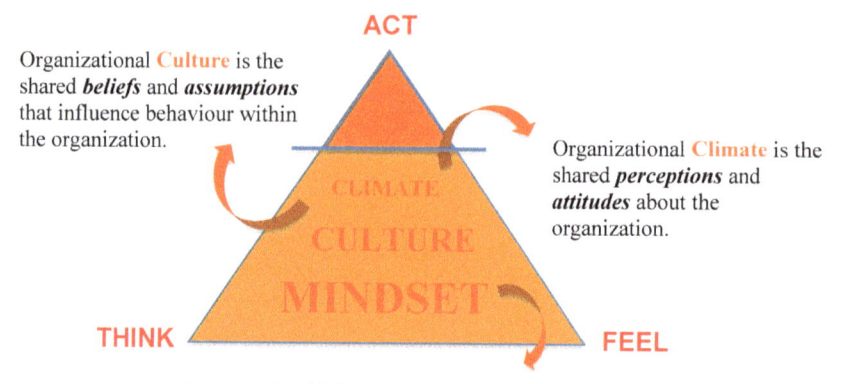

Organizational **Culture** is the shared ***beliefs*** and ***assumptions*** that influence behaviour within the organization.

Organizational **Climate** is the shared ***perceptions*** and ***attitudes*** about the organization.

Organizational **Mindset** embodies the values, beliefs, and thinking preferences that influence attention and action.

An organization's mindset, particularly as it is measured within the OGI, is interrelated with culture and climate, but is distinguished from these elements by the articulation of the organization's unique cognitive style. A cognitive style is a psychological dimension that is generally viewed as a preferred approach to processing information, decision making, addressing tasks, and solving problems. Importantly, "it concerns individual differences in the processes of *cognition*, which generally include all processes by which knowledge is acquired: perception, thought, memory, imagery…and problem solving."[52] *

Mindset is an active and dynamic expression of an organization's culture, in that it taps into underlying values, beliefs, and assumptions at play within it. Mindset is distinct from culture, however, in that it also sheds light on the organization's unique cognitive stylistic preferences, which shape strategy formulation, and the way in which resources and talent are harnessed. Each organization possesses a unique cognitive style, which is quantified within the OGI by the extent to which it leverages each of the 4 Principal Mindsets.

---

* See also, Jerry Rhodes and Sue Thame, *The Colours of Your Mind*; Jerry Rhodes, *Conceptual Toolmaking*; and Jerry Rhodes, *I Wonder: The Science of Imagination*.

Mapping Your Organization's Mindset

Your organization's mindset can be mapped by utilizing the following model.

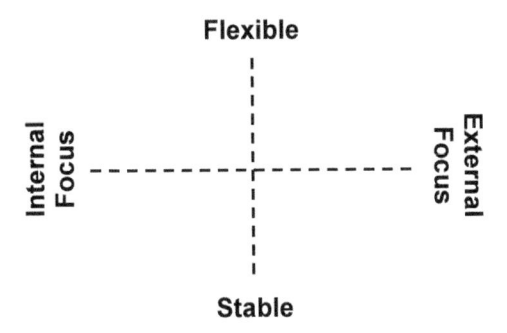

```
                    Flexible
                       |
                       |
      Internal    -----+-----    External
      Focus           |           Focus
                       |
                       |
                    Stable
```

The model positions each of the 4 Principal Mindsets onto what is called the Competing Values Framework, originally developed by Robert Quinn and John Rohrbraugh,[53] which helps codify organizations along two continuums: *Flexible vs. Stable*, and *Internal Focus vs. External Focus*. It is helpful to think of these continuums as representing dynamic tensions that exist within most organizations as they strive to achieve intelligent action.

No one end of either continuum is better than the other, *per se*, although some may be more adaptive depending on the kinds of challenges the organization is facing at any given time in its lifecycle. In actuality, successful organizations will be those that are effective at balancing and appropriately leveraging these dimensions in their efforts to achieve long-term viability and sustained success.

- *Flexible* organizations will be more open to changing processes and structures, valuing agility and responsiveness to meeting new and emerging needs of stakeholders, partners, and customers.
- *Stable* organizations will be more focused on maintaining a consistent, routinized approach to meeting the needs of the business and its customers.
- *Externally focused* organizations are more sensitive and responsive to shifts occurring in their external operating environment, for example with competitors and changing market dynamics.

- *Internally focused* organizations are more sensitive and responsive to their internal operating environment, for example the extent to which talent, strategies, processes, and systems are aligned to achieve optimal results.

In a similar fashion as Kim Cameron and Robert Quinn mapped their four culture types onto the Competing Values Framework,[54] we are now able to integrate the 4 Principal Mindsets — Imagine, Resolve, Analyze, and Align — within the corresponding dimensions of the competing values framework.

Mapping Your Organization's Mindset

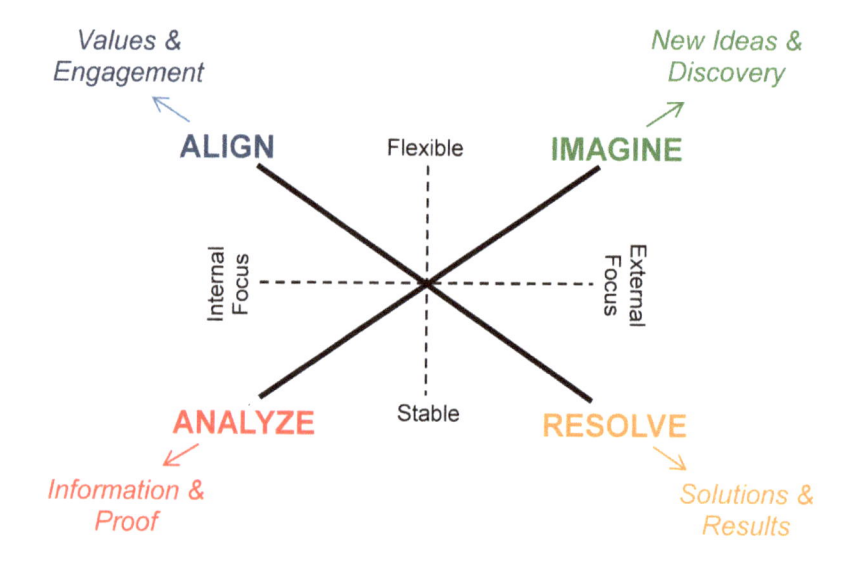

```
      Values &                                New Ideas &
      Engagement                              Discovery
           ↖                                      ↗
        ALIGN          Flexible          IMAGINE
                     Internal │ External
                     Focus    │ Focus
                     - - - - -┼- - - - -
        ANALYZE        Stable           RESOLVE
           ↙                                      ↘
      Information &                          Solutions &
      Proof                                  Results
```

- The **IMAGINE** Mindset with its focus on new ideas and discovery combines flexibility with an external focus.

- The **RESOLVE** Mindset with its focus on solutions and results combines stability with an external focus.

- The **ANALYZE** Mindset with its focus on information and proof combines stability with an internal focus.

- The **ALIGN** Mindset with its focus on values and integration combines flexibility with an internal focus.

You are now in a position to map the extent to which your organization leverages each of these 4 Mindsets, which influence its ability to grow and thrive through change.

The Mindset of Your Organization

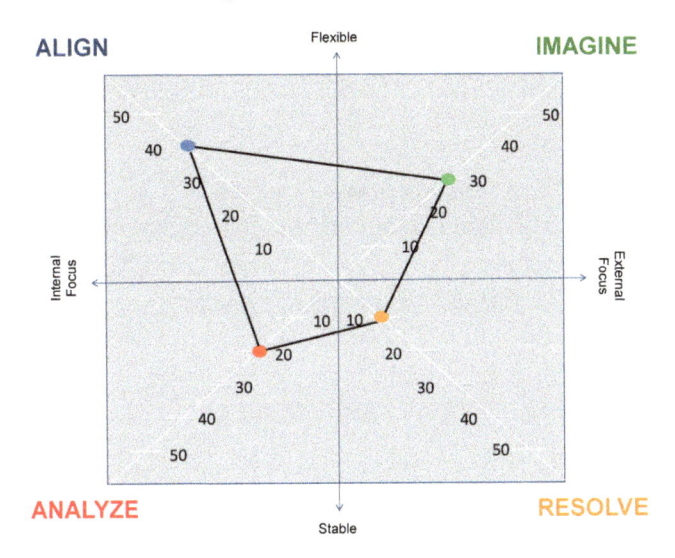

Part One: Your Organization's Current Mindset

Reflecting on the current state of your organization, how it dominantly thinks, feels and acts, distribute 100 percent between the 4 Mindsets on the grid, according to what you believe to be the relative strength of match with your organization. By way of example only, you might distribute the scores for your organization as follows: Align = 40%, Imagine = 30%, Resolve = 10%, Analyze = 20% (Total = 100%).

Having plotted the relative scores for your organization, you can then connect the dots to formulate a visual diagram that depicts the unique, overarching mindset for your organization. Using the hypothetical example above, you can see that this organization maintains a strong internal focus, unified by shared values and strategic integration (**ALIGN**), while leveraging systems, policies and internal controls to ensure evidence-based decision making (**ANALYZE**). Boeing could potentially be a company that would possess this overall mindset.

Having done this with numerous leaders within organizations, it is helpful for them to utilize this common language and tool to share, dialogue, and explore the implications related to the differences and similarities between their mindset diagrams they have created. It is also enlightening for leaders to compare the differences between various departments, divisions, and business units within their organizations as it sheds light on the way in which mindsets are reflective of the unique strategies, business challenges, leadership styles, and subcultures that exist within their organizations.

Inconvenient Truth #4
The goals of organizations and the goals of innovation are most often the same and yet the two are experienced by organizational members as enemies, not allies.

Part Two: Your Organization's Future Mindset

Having mapped the current mindset of your organization, it is equally instructive to reflect on where specifically, and to what degree, will your organization's mindset need to shift in order to sustain future success. The second part of the exercise is important as it stimulates proactive thinking and problem solving between leaders focused on identifying tangible strategies and actions that will promote growth, organizational effectiveness, and adaptive change. I ask leaders to use a dotted line or different colour overlaid onto the "current state" Mindset map to create what they believe to be the most adaptive "future" Mindset for their organizations.

The key questions to be asked, relating to each of the 4 Principal Mindsets for your organization to achieve mid- to long-term viability, are:

1. Does this mindset need to be magnified? If so, by how much? In what ways?
2. Does this mindset need to be minimized? If so, by how much? In what ways?
3. Is the mindset appropriate where it is? If so, what is required to sustain it?

Using the previous example, the hypothetical organization may need to magnify its IMAGINE and RESOLVE Mindsets in order to be more nimble, agile and responsive to external, competitive threats and/or shifting customer needs and demands.

What's Your Organization's Type

To add another layer of dimensionality to the exploration of your organization's mindset, I have identified 4 Core Organizational Types that can be associated with distinct combinations of the 4 Principal Mindsets. While many organizations are not just one pure type, and there indeed many different variations and "types" of organizations, I've nevertheless identified these as "core" Organizational Types: *Entrepreneurial, Competitive, Bureaucratic,* and *Societal*. It is instructive to gauge the extent to which your organization's unique, overall mindset corresponds with the values, philosophies, and goals of these Core Organizational Types.

4 Core Organizational Types Matched with 4 Principal Mindsets

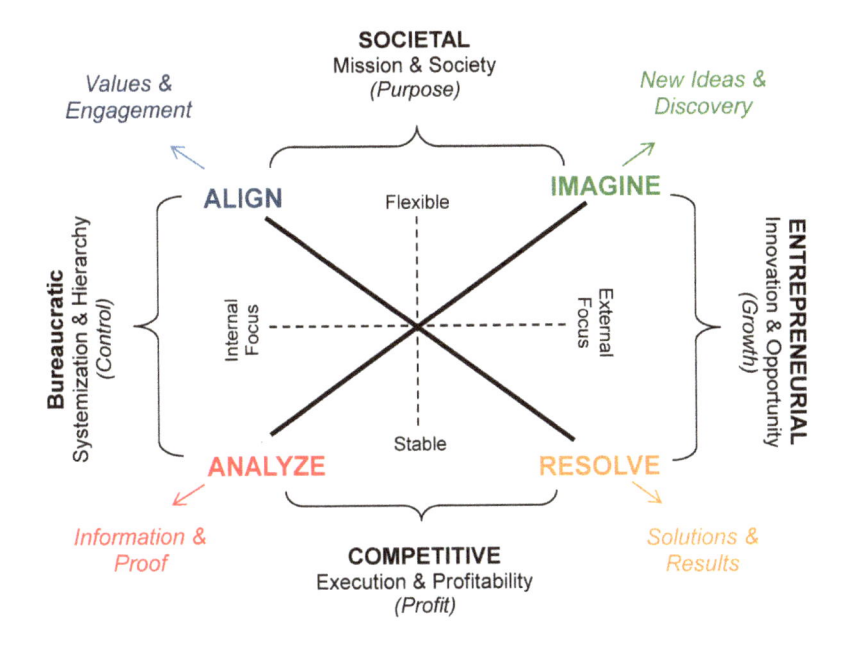

Values & Engagement

SOCIETAL
Mission & Society
(Purpose)

New Ideas & Discovery

ALIGN   Flexible   **IMAGINE**

Bureaucratic
Systemization & Hierarchy
(Control)

Internal Focus — External Focus

ENTREPRENEURIAL
Innovation & Opportunity
(Growth)

ANALYZE   Stable   **RESOLVE**

Information & Proof

COMPETITIVE
Execution & Profitability
(Profit)

Solutions & Results

Entrepreneurial Organizations: (A synthesis of **IMAGINE** and **RESOLVE**) organizations seeking growth through innovation promote flexibility, creativity, and risk-taking. The main currency within Entrepreneurial type organizations is "growth," meaning that organizational attention and energy is focused on creating and developing new ideas, knowledge, products, and services that will accelerate growth for the company. Growth is what gets measured, what is valued, and what is rewarded.

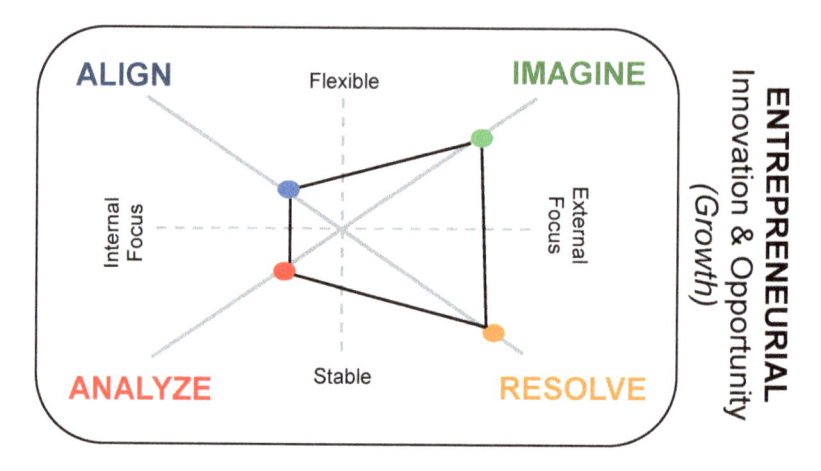

[Diagram: A quadrant chart with ALIGN (top-left), IMAGINE (top-right), ANALYZE (bottom-left), RESOLVE (bottom-right). Axes labeled Flexible/Stable (vertical) and Internal Focus/External Focus (horizontal). Right side labeled ENTREPRENEURIAL — Innovation & Opportunity (Growth).]

Examples

Most "start-ups" could be classified as entrepreneurial. Although even some more mature organizations manage to maintain an entrepreneurial mindset. Think of Apple when Steve Jobs was at the helm. Some examples of other innovative organizations would include: Uber and Tesla in transportation, Alibaba in e-commerce, Google in web-based search (and Waymo — self-driving cars), Chobani in food, Gilead Sciences in biotech, Netflix in entertainment, Airbnb in travel, IBM for giving us Watson, and Amazon in, well, many things in including e-commerce.

Competitive Organizations: (A synthesis of **RESOLVE** and **ANALYZE**) organizations focused on profitability promote productivity, efficiency, and execution. The main currency within competitive type organizations is "profit," meaning that the bottom line is the prime mover. Maximizing efficiencies and margins, and achieving a strong ROI for shareholders is what's rewarded.

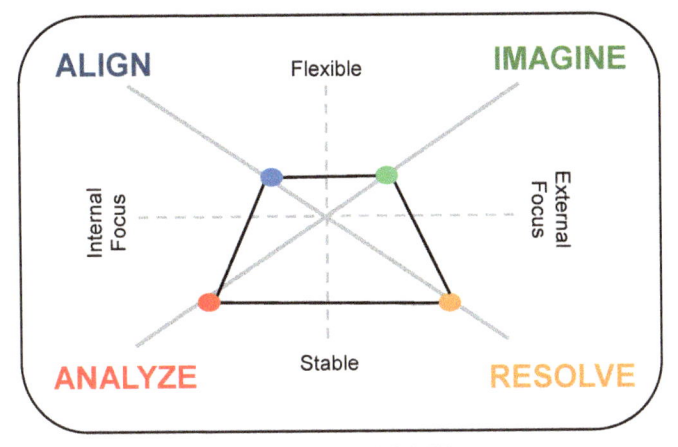

```
ALIGN          Flexible         IMAGINE


  Internal                       External
  Focus                          Focus



ANALYZE         Stable          RESOLVE
```

COMPETITIVE
Execution & Profitability
(Profit)

Most "Blue Chip" organizations could be considered competitive type organizations. Some that stand out would include: all banking institutions (such as JP Morgan Chase, HSBC, RBC and the Bank of China), Berkshire Hathaway in investing and insurance, Walmart in retail, General Electric (GE) in various sectors including aviation and energy, 3G Capital in global investing, and The Blackstone Group in private equity.

Bureaucratic Organizations: (A synthesis of **ANALYZE** and **ALIGN**) organizations focused on hierarchy and control promote rules, procedures, and systemization. The main currency within Bureaucratic type organizations is "control," meaning that hierarchic power, levels of authority, discipline, and conformity to established rules and principles is what is rewarded and valued.

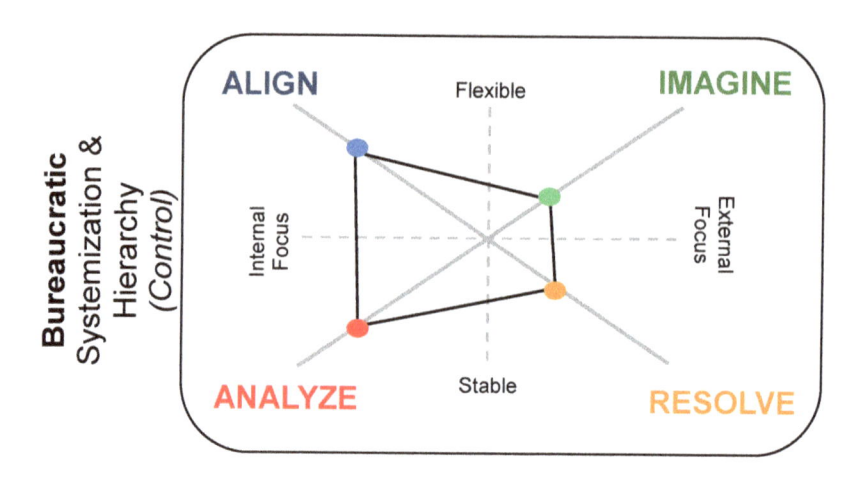

Examples

Most government institutions function as bureaucracies, Washington's Congress comes to mind. All military groups such as the Navy, Army, Airforce, and Marines operate along very clear lines of command and control leadership hierarchies. Some large "for-profit" companies could also be considered bureaucratic, such as Boeing and Airbus in the aerospace industry or Union Pacific and Canadian National in the railroad industry.

Societal Organizations: (A Synthesis of **ALIGN** and **IMAGINE**) organizations focused on humanity promote the betterment of people, society, and/or environment. The main currency within Societal type organizations is "purpose," meaning the galvanizing focus within the organization centers around the fulfillment of its philanthropic or egalitarian vision. Alignment to the societal values embedded within the organization's purpose is what is valued and rewarded by members.

SOCIETAL
Mission & Society
(Purpose)

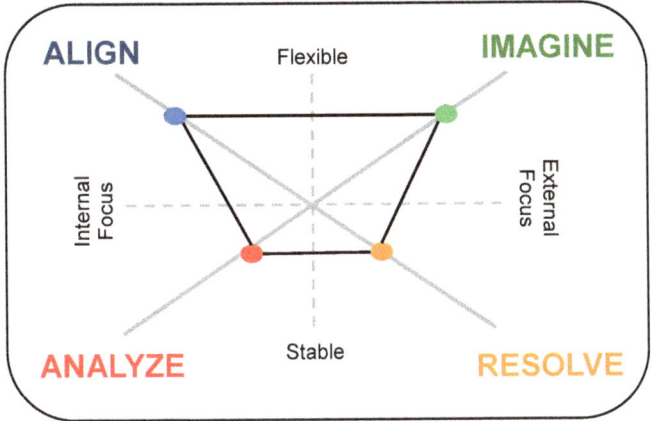

```
ALIGN          Flexible           IMAGINE

Internal                                 External
Focus                                    Focus

ANALYZE        Stable             RESOLVE
```

Examples

World Vision International, with its focus on overcoming poverty and injustice throughout the world, would be a good example. UNESCO (United Nations Educational, Scientific, and Cultural Organization) with its focus on "building peace in the minds of men and women" through its support of global initiatives such as improving access to quality education for adults and children, fostering freedom of expression and activities to support sustainable development is another good example of a societally focused organization. Some others would include: Greenpeace International, The Salvation Army, the Sierra Club, and the Nature Conservancy.

*****

An organization's dominant cognitive style, identified by the extent to which it embraces and indeed leverages the 4 Principal Mindsets, is linked to what it values and how it seeks to fulfill its purpose and mission as an organization. Even though an organization's culture may be somewhat stable and enduring, by surfacing its Mindset with the OGI, leaders can tangibly pinpoint and magnify the adaptive elements within their organization's culture. In parallel, leaders can develop practical strategies to shift the way organizational members think, feel and act in order to achieve adaptive action and sustained organizational success.

Mindset is a tangible expression of the organization's culture and is an integral element of the organization's internal environment. As we have seen, different types of organizations seem to possess more pronounced expressions of certain mindsets over others. In our experience, however, we have found that organizations who are effective at leveraging each of the 4 Principal Mindsets will experience higher levels of growth and will have a greater ability to achieve adaptive change. It's now time to explore why that is by demonstrating examples of how they impact organizations like yours.

Chapter 4 References

50. The Conference Board. *CEO Challenge 2015 Research Report*, revised February 11, 2015.

51. Sacks, Jonathon. *The Great Partnership: God, Science and the Search for Meaning.* London, UK: Hodder and Stoughton, 2011.

52. Ausburn, Lynna and Floyd Ausburn, (1978). "Cognitive styles: Some information and implications for instructional design." *Educational Communication & Technology*, 26(4), 337-354. See also Robert Sternberg, Jerry Rhodes, and Gerard Puccio.

53. Quinn, Robert and John Rohrbraugh. "A Spatial Model of Effectiveness Criteria: Toward a Competing Values Approach to Organization Analysis," *Management Science*, 1983, 29: 363-377.

54. Cameron, Kim and Robert Quinn. *Diagnosing and Changing Organizational Culture: Based on the Competing Values Framework*. 3rd ed. San Francisco, CA: Jossey-Bass, 2011.

CHAPTER 5

The Transformation Wheel®

The OGI Score is not just a typological description of your organization's culture, it's also a measure indicating your organization's actual ability to grow and change in adaptive ways.

Getting the wheels of growth and transformation moving within your organization

Later in this chapter, we will explore the elements within The Transformation Wheel, but let's begin with the end first. The end game of growth and transformation is better effectiveness and results. Leaders are tasked with positioning their organizations for greater success, and yet they are often lacking tangible, valid data that provides a true reading on their organization's current readiness for change.

In the first chapter, I introduced the OGI Scoring Index. Now you'll see that I've added another dimension on the bottom row that indicates expected revenue growth rates associated with each of the 5 Tier Ratings.

Figure 5: The OGI Scoring Index

OGI Growth & Transformation Tier Rating	Tier 5	Tier 4	Tier 3	Tier 2	Tier 1
OGI Overall Scoring Range – %	≥66%	65 – 57%	56 – 48%	47 – 39%	≤38%
Overall "Stance" to the Operating Environment	Pre-emptive	Proactive	Mixed	Reactive	Non-responsive
Ability to Grow through New Value Creation	Advanced	Proficient	Moderate	Marginal	Poor
Ability to Effectively Change	Excelling	Thriving	Adapting	Developing	Lagging
POTENTIAL GROWTH CAPABILITY Actual Revenue and other relevant KPI's – (Key Performance Indicators)	≥ 25%	24 – 10%	9 – 1%	0 – (-8) %	≤ (-9) %

As you can see on the OGI Scoring Index, higher OGI scores equate to higher levels of adaptiveness to change and a greater capability to achieve higher levels of real revenue growth.

Shortly, we will explore some actual examples of the OGI in action with several organizations, and see how their OGI scores correlated with their actual revenue performance in line with the Scoring Index. Leaders interested in shifting their organization's cultural mindset to enhance growth and performance can leverage the OGI to gauge where their organization is now and pinpoint what particular levers they need to pull to initiate their transformational vision. Shifting an organization's culture is no easy task. However, with a validated tool and common language, leaders can simplify the complex task of cultural transformation.

Inconvenient Truth #10
There is a dramatic need to better understand the relationship between organizational thinking and organizational innovation.

The Transformation Wheel

Understanding and leveraging the most critical elements that influence an organization's ability to grow and transform adaptively is integral knowledge for every leader, particularly those leaders interested in stimulating growth. The twelve specific, research-based elements that are assessed within the OGI are situated on what is called The Transformation Wheel (see Figure 6). You'll see how the 4 Principal Mindsets, which we've already addressed, are situated on the model and now you can see the 8 Orientations that serve to complete the Transformation Wheel. I'm sure you can identify any number of reasons (and analogies) for why I've given it that particular name. For example:

- Keeping the wheels of innovation moving forward, and of course, the wheel was among the first great inventions.

- The tires on your car are best when they have the right air pressure, but when they are low, your vehicle doesn't corner very well, and your car will not be able to reach its maximum speed.

Similarly, your organization's "growth engine" will be optimized when all of the elements within The Transformation Wheel are firing on all cylinders and are in sync with each other. It is when some of the elements within the wheel are either overused, underused, or even ignored that your organization's growth engine underperforms.

Figure 6: The Transformation Wheel

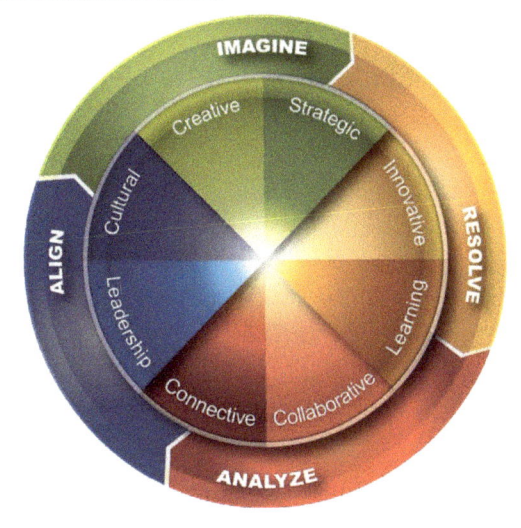

The twelve dimensions assessed within the OGI are situated on The Transformation Wheel, which I refer to as a "systems-based" model for a couple of reasons. First, all organizations are systems. More specifically, I suggest they are *cognitive systems* in that they are purposeful, adaptive, and selective — they only construct meaning from information they select as significant from their internal and external environments in their adaptive efforts.

Secondly, innovation occurring within organizations is a *whole system phenomenon*. As with all systems, it's the interrelationships and interactions between the elements within the system that constitute the essential nature of an organizational system. In other words, we can only know, understand, and indeed meaningfully influence an organizational system by way of a holistic analysis of the elements interacting within it. If we are to understand an organization's true innovative capability, we need to understand how different factors (such as leadership, culture, strategy) within the organizational system are influencing each other.

The Transformation Wheel is intended to depict the systemic and holistic relationships existing among the key elements that influence growth and transformation within all organizations, including your own.

The 8 Orientations

The 8 factors derived through in-depth research are referred to as "Orientations" because they steer and shape an organization's approach to growth. Each Orientation within the OGI is designed to capture people's experiences and perceptions regarding actual behaviours, actions, and activities that are (or are not) occurring within the organization and influencing its ability to grow through innovation and adaptive change.

The IMAGINE Mindset supports the
Creative and *Strategic* Orientations

- Loosening up the rigidity of ingrained assumptions
- Seeing things differently and seeing new things
- Visualizing what's required for future success

1. Creative Orientation

Creativity is a key ingredient in the process of developing fresh ideas that lead to innovative improvements of any kind. Without a novel idea, it is difficult to move beyond the status quo. At its root, growth through innovation is fundamentally a goal-directed process intended to improve the status quo by enhancing existing products, processes, and/or services. In this age of increased complexity and ambiguity, creativity is largely recognized by researchers and business leaders alike as an essential skill set and organizational capability needed to remain competitive and relevant.

For example, at the 2016 World Economic Forum held in Davos-Klosters, Switzerland, global leaders explored the top ten essential skills necessary for success in the workplace in 2020. They concluded that creativity ranked among the top three.[55] The 2010, *IBM Global CEO Study*, titled "Capitalizing on Complexity," which included over 1500 CEOs, general managers and senior public sector leaders from sixty countries and thirty-three industries, concluded that "creativity is the most important leadership quality."[56]

Harvard professor Theresa Amabile, along with her research collaborators, contends that "all innovation begins with creative ideas," and importantly, they also suggest that within an organizational context, creativity is not solely determined by the level of skill or innate strengths individuals may possess: "the social environment can influence both the level and the frequency of creative behaviour."[57]

This is exactly why organizational innovation ought to be viewed as a *whole-system phenomenon* because creativity, among other factors, is influenced by an array of dynamics operating within the whole organizational system, such as cultural and leadership elements that may either support or constrain creative thinking and behaviour.

The Creative Orientation captures the processes, skills, and cultural dynamics currently existing within an organization that are nurturing and promoting the creativity of individuals and teams in the service of innovation.

An attempt to assess an organization's ability to grow requires an understanding of how it encourages and develops individual and team creativity within the organization. Importantly, creativity is a necessary, but not a sufficient condition, for organizations as cognitive systems to achieve intelligent action through innovation and adaptive change.

Some key questions for you to ask yourself related to your organization's *Creative* Orientation:

- To what extent are we encouraged to challenge organizational practices?
- To what extent does our organization and culture enable creative thinking?
- To what extent are leaders and key contributors encouraged to take responsible risks?

2. Strategic Orientation

Strategy is an overt reflection of how an organization thinks, what it values, and what it chooses to pay attention to in its environment. And by "environment" I mean, in keeping with Arie De Geus, "the sum total of all the forces that affect a company's actions."[58] Strategy, by definition, ought to be future focused, which means leaders are required to tune in to their operating environment. They require foresight — a sensitivity to both see and acknowledge signals of significance emerging from their environment, which could have a material affect on their company's ability to achieve intelligent action in the future.

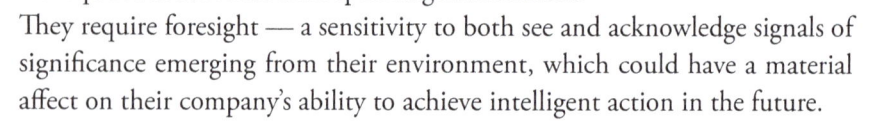

Successful organizations are those that are able to effectively shape, execute, and adjust their strategies — and associated structures and processes — in a world of continuous change and disruption. Strategy is integral to growth through innovation as it sets the direction in which creative energy, knowledge generation, and innovation efforts will be focused. For instance, Kim and Mauborgne explore the notion of "value innovation" and the fundamental requirement that an organization's innovation agenda be tightly connected to its core strategic focus. Implicit within value innovation, for example, which they label as "blue ocean strategy," is a whole-system approach to make value innovation viable, otherwise the "innovation will remain divided from the core of strategy."[59]

A negative consequence of this is that organizational members can get confused about the relevance of the proposed innovative initiatives. This can happen when the organizational conditions (such as managerial support and resources) needed to support those innovation initiatives are diluted and/or redirected to other more urgent activities required to achieve the organization's "core" business objectives. The clear message sent to organizational members is that the short-term needs of the business override innovative activities that require a mid- to long-term approach.

Of course, flexibility needs to be present with respect to shifting resources around to meet the monthly operational needs of the business. However, when this becomes a chronic organizational response pattern, it does not bode well for growth through innovation.

Given that an organization's strategic focus is — or ought to be — tightly connected to its innovation strategy, it is important to understand the cognitive approach, if not biases influencing the sense-making activities of the strategy-makers/leaders within the organization. I suggest that the way an organization shapes its strategies, via its leaders, offers insight into the way in which the organization, as a cognitive system, observes its environment, or rather, what information the organization *chooses* as meaningful within its environment.

The Strategic Orientation captures the level of strategic sensitivity and flexibility to external change, and *how* the organization currently responds strategically to change within its external environment. This orientation captures the extent to which innovation is tangibly integrated into the fabric of the organization's overall strategic agenda.

Some key questions for you to ask yourself related to your organization's *Strategic* Orientation

- To what extent is your organization capable of adapting to market conditions?

- To what extent can your organization shift its structure and processes to meet emerging needs and demands?
- To what extent does your organization effectively link its innovation agenda to the business or overall organizational strategy?

Lessons from the Research Field – Creative and Strategic Orientations

Applying the OGI within organizations, leaders indicated:

A. The CREATIVE Orientation was shown to be the least-developed orientation and it was deemed (by research participants) to be influenced primarily by the LEADERSHIP, CULTURAL, and INNOVATIVE Orientations.

B. It was often connected to motivation and engagement. Rather than it being a skill deficit, the CREATIVE Orientation was often thought to be low either because the leadership or the culture did not reinforce or stimulate creative thought.

C. A learning related to the STRATEGIC Orientation revolved around the importance of actually possessing an innovation strategy, particularly one that was integrated into the organization's overall strategic agenda.

D. Results indicated that it is important for organizations to first be clear on the definition of innovation. And second, to be clear on the types of innovation relevant for their particular organization.

The RESOLVE Mindset supports
the *Innovative* and *Learning* Orientations

- Transforming good ideas into value-added solutions
- Overcoming resistances and obstacles
- Gaining insight from successes and failures

3. Innovative Orientation

For 943 CEOs, globally, innovation ranked number two in the top five strategies to sustain their organization's success, according to the Conference Board, CEO 2015 Research Report.[60] Innovation is repeatedly reported as the engine for survival, particularly in this era of rapid technological innovation. Despite the fact that CEOs and executives intuitively "get it," many still struggle with how to "do it" or do it better.

Enhancing your organization's growth engine starts with an understanding that innovation is largely influenced by your organization's inner environment, which includes its *cultural mindset*. For example, in the CEO study cited above, enhancing innovation requires first and foremost "creating a culture of innovation by promoting and rewarding entrepreneurship and risk taking."

A reason this is critically important is that innovation requires people to think differently. However, it also requires people to stick their necks out, to be bold, to persevere — and these actions can feel personally risky to leaders and key contributors. If the environment within the organization presents cultural cues that suggest challenging the status quo is too "career" or socially threatening, would-be innovators will keep their great ideas and passion to themselves, limiting the organization's growth capability. This is why I contend in Inconvenient Truth #13 that "innovation is every bit emotional as intellectual for every member of the organization."

Enhancing organizational innovation also requires leaders to engage in "both/and" thinking to avoid being caught in the paralyzing, damned-if I-do/damned-if-I-don't Catch-22 situation. On the one hand, organizations require operational competence, which focuses leadership attention toward short-term, repeatable, and predictable business processes that are needed to maximize resources and drive profitability. On the other hand, innovation requires leaders to step outside of what is predictable or what feels certain given the ambiguous and somewhat risky outcomes of innovation ventures that "might" create future wealth and prosperity for the business.

Roger Martin, former Dean of the Rotman School of Business, describes this Catch-22 paradox in a similar fashion although he frames it as a difference between a cognitive focus (if not bias) between "reliability" versus "validity." Martin suggests the "goal of reliability is to produce consistent, predictable outcomes…[whereas] the goal of validity, on the other hand, is to produce outcomes that meet desired objectives."[61] The dominant cultural mindset of the organization will strongly influence the type of thinking and behaviour that's reinforced and rewarded.

In reality, both of the opposing perspectives are needed to achieve sustained, long-term success for most organizations. Leaders will benefit by both focusing on daily operations with an emphasis on achieving reliable predictions to meet monthly profit targets and pursuing innovations that require shifting organizational resources away from predictable routines, yet position the organization for future success.

It is clear that innovation involves transforming ideas and knowledge into new or better products, processes, and/or services. At a more macro level, innovation also supports organizations in their efforts to transform from their current state to a better state, which improves the organization's ability to secure long-term viability and success. The Innovative orientation captures the degree to which innovation is currently valued, resourced, developed, and executed within the organization.

Some key questions for you to ask yourself
related to your organization's
Innovative Orientation

- To what extent is your organization successful at implementing new ideas?
- To what extent does your organization's cultural mindset support innovation?
- To what extent are your leaders capable of both/and thinking?

4. Learning Orientation

Learning is what the system does to transform its environment."
— Von Foerster

Learning is woven into the very fabric of innovation and growth. Given innovation and growth means doing new things, it is essentially impossible to do new things without learning new things, or at least seeing things in new and different ways. From an organizational perspective, learning is critical to keeping up with shifting customer values and requirements, as well as jumping ahead of existing competitors and new entrants who are actively seeking ways to erode your customer base and disrupt your existing business model. The importance of learning cannot be overemphasized. If innovation is the engine, learning is the fuel. Without it, you'll go nowhere in a hurry. Organizations not only need to get good at learning, they need to find ways to learn faster and more effectively.

Organizational learning is strongly related to organizational innovation in business literature. There are many examples, but here are just a few. Jeffrey Pfeffer, for example, aligns learning with innovation as he explores what is involved in making organizations smarter. He contends that "brainpower and skills are what matter, and nurturing the capacity for innovation and invention is not only a sound investment, it is essential for companies' success."[62] John Seely Brown and Paul Duguid suggest that "working, learning, and innovating are closely related forms of human activity."[63] James March explored the notion of organizational learning and its relationship to the dichotomous innovation strategies of exploitation *vs.* exploration.[64]

Peter Senge's now classic book, *The Fifth Discipline*, was dedicated to the practice of learning within organizations. For Senge, a learning organization is "an organization that is continuously expanding its capacity to create its future."[65] Learning is linked to an organization's ability to shape its future success. Here we see learning clearly linked to your organization's current and future competitive edge. Think about it, the totality of human knowledge is doubling on average every thirteen months or less. With the onslaught of the knowledge explosion where, according to IBM, the build out of the "Internet of Things" will lead to the doubling of knowledge every eleven hours,[66] it isn't too hard to see why learning is critical to organizational survival. In fact, now in this new world order, we have to learn how to learn better, differently, and faster.

The *Learning* Orientation within the OGI therefore captures the degree to which information and knowledge are captured and shared between individuals, teams, and functions within the organization. It also assesses the degree to which learning is valued and used as a critical enabler of an organization's ability to innovate and transform effectively.

Some key questions for you to ask yourself related to your organization's *Learning* Orientation

- To what extent does your organization value learning as a strategic imperative?
- To what extent does your organization meaningfully connect learning to innovation and growth?
- To what extent does your organization capture and leverage lessons learned?

Lessons from the Research Field – Innovative and *Learning Orientations*

Applying the OGI within organizations, leaders indicated:

A. Aside from the tangible impact failure to innovate can have on an organization's performance, an unintended (and less immediately apparent) consequence is the impact that chronically stalled or disbanded innovation efforts can have on the spirit of the firm.

B. Failure to select appropriate innovations aligned with the firm's overall strategic agenda can lead to ineffective execution as innovation leaders and teams struggle with competing interests, and resources are pulled away from the innovation project to serve more "immediate" operational needs.

C. Under conditions where short-term, operational thinking trumps long-term innovative thinking, organizational learning appears to be diluted. In effect, organizational memory is short term, therefore, potentially valuable learnings acquired from previous innovation experiences are not available or easily accessed for retrieval to support current and future innovations.

D. Results indicated that organizational learning is connected to its ability to remain open and responsive to change. The processes of learning and innovation are inextricably linked to an organization's adaptive capability.

The ANALYZE Mindset supports
the *Collaborative* and *Connective* Orientations

- Bringing together diverse knowledge sources
- Leveraging facts and information for evidence-based decisions
- Accelerating the connectivity and flow of ideas and knowledge

5. Collaborative Orientation

Real collaboration involves more than just people getting along together and "playing nice." At its best, collaboration generates *creative tension* between individuals with diverse cognitive styles and experiences who maintain a shared interest in solving a clearly defined problem. As such, collaboration is a dynamic and often messy process, which often involves emotionally charged exchanges between "collaborators" as they seek to achieve mutually desirable outcomes.

According to many business leaders, collaboration is an indispensable discipline embedded within the innovation process and yet many admit that their organizations could be doing it much better. This is consistent with a study conducted by the Conference Board of Canada,[67] where 24.5 percent of 222 leaders indicated that a barrier to their organizations innovating more was "a lack of in-house expertise." In my experience, working with many organizations at a global level, I have witnessed a meaningful gap between the perceived need (and desire) to collaborate and innovate and the skills required to actually execute these disciplines well.

While improved collaboration is required within organizations, more and more collaborations must occur with stakeholders outside of the organization. Henry Chesbrough has created a compelling argument that in fact a new paradigm, *open innovation*, is required to adapt to the new and emerging realities of globalization and the technological revolution.

Organizations that utilize traditional models of innovation are more closed in that they enact a mindset that sources knowledge primarily from within the company, to keep intellectual property, such as patents away from others, and resist the use of externally sourced technologies. Under such a model, projects are solely initiated by the R&D team and a portion of projects are funnelled through to the market for direct introduction by the firm. Chesbrough refers to this approach as a "closed" innovation model because "projects can only enter in one way, at the beginning, and can only exit in one way, by going into the market."[68]

An open *innovation model*, on the other hand, is more dynamic, less linear, and more open to acquiring or borrowing knowledge, ideas, and technologies from sources outside of the firm. There are three compelling aspects of Chesbrough's open innovation paradigm that are relevant to this research:

1. The landscape has changed and requires a subsequent shift in mindset to innovate effectively within this new landscape.

2. Its utility is seen best through the lens of radical innovation (RI), which requires a managerial approach that is sympathetic to systems thinking and a commensurate belief in the need to systemically integrate innovation within the organization's business model.

3. Collaborative innovation is an essential capability that requires greater focus no matter what innovation model is being utilized: open, closed, or otherwise.

4. An exploration of a number of theorists (and theories) including Chesbrough, when connected begin to show a new pattern of innovation that is necessary to survive in the 21st century. Steven Johnson in his book, *Where Good Ideas Come From*, shares a meta-analysis of key innovations starting from the 14th century and categorizes these innovations into four quadrants. He argues that the fourth quadrant is the most prevalent and necessary as it "corresponds to open-source or academic environments, where ideas can be built upon and re-imagined in large collaborative networks."[69]

The most significant shift in innovation, he argues, is the movement away from the individual to the group: "Less than 10% of innovation during the Renaissance [was] networked; two centuries later, a majority of breakthrough ideas emerge[d] in collaborative environments." As Friedman suggests, "the development of a global, web-enabled playing field [has allowed] for multiple forms of collaboration — the sharing of knowledge and work — in real time, without regard to geography, distance, or, in the near future, even language."[70]

Globalization has shifted the context in which organizations produce value and indeed compete. In parallel with globalization, technological innovation has both enabled and precipitated the need to collaborate with others across disciplines and now geographies to adapt and respond to relentless competitive pressures and shifting market forces.

Organizations need the appropriate skills, mindset, and processes to drive effective innovation. Among those skills is a competence to enact real collaboration, not just with outside partners but also with individuals and teams internally across the enterprise. Getting knowledge, ideas, and talent connected both within the organization and with external partners in such a way that allows for greater degrees of collaboration is essential for organizations that wish to thrive in the 21st century.

The majority of innovations now occur through collaborations between multiple stakeholders within and beyond the organization. The Collaborative Orientation captures the extent to which collaboration is maximized internally within teams and across functions, as well as with external partners to support innovation and effective action.

Some key questions for you to ask yourself related to your organization's *Collaborative* Orientation

- To what extent do we enable constructive debate in our organization?
- To what extent do we leverage external stakeholders to enhance our innovative capability and output as an organization?
- To what extent do teams leverage diverse cognitive styles to improve creative problem solving and decision making?

6. Connective Orientation

"Chance favours the connected mind."
– Steven Johnson

Organizations as cognitive systems are intelligent to the extent that they can leverage their connective capability. At an individual or leader level, being "connective" refers to an openness and intent to reach out, to explore, learn, and grow. At an organizational level, it refers to the presence of systems, processes, and tools that are leveraged to drive innovation and growth.

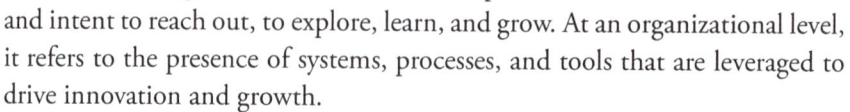

Given the advent of the new informational, global economy described by Manuel Castells, organizations are and will increasingly be required to advance their abilities to leverage external networks to keep pace with technological change. Castells argues that "cooperation and networking offer the only possibility of sharing costs and risks, as well as keeping up with constantly renewed information."[71]

While the Connective and Collaborative Orientations are related, they do present distinct factors that influence an organization's ability to innovate and grow. It is necessary but not sufficient for an organization to experience high levels of collaboration within functional or even cross-functional units. Organizations are now required to maintain an organizational structure — or cognitive architecture — that enables and encourages the cross-pollination of information, ideas, and knowledge across and beyond the boundaries of the organization by utilizing information technologies and networks.

Mark Granovetter*, for example, introduced the notion of "weak ties" within social networks, which is relevant given organizations consist of an array of embedded networks along with connective relationships that exist between the nodes, hubs, and clusters within those networks.

The concept of weak ties speaks to the advantage of connecting with people outside of your usual professional circles or communities where you enjoy

---

* See Mark Granovetter, *The Strength of Weak Ties: Network Theory Revisited, Sociological Theory 1 (1983):* 201-233.

strong ties. They are considered "strong" because they likely fall within your community of practice, where you share similar education and professional interests and experiences. "Weak ties," on the other hand, represent opportunities to reach out and connect with people who are less familiar, and who likely think differently than you. Granovetter suggests that these weak tie connections offer the greatest potential to trigger new insights and promote innovative thinking.

Being connective, then, suggests the active and intentional search for novelty given an underlying belief that random environments and serendipitous exchanges can stimulate new ideas. Even within organizations, different units can stand alone and indeed have autonomous or even conflicting goals. However, strengthening existing connections and making new connections between the subsystems can stimulate new channels for novelty to occur, thereby greatly increasing their value to the organization beyond the business unit's purely functional or operational mandate.

Organizational leaders and members require motivation and willpower to reach beyond their business units to meaningfully collaborate cross-functionally, as well as with external partners, which is particularly challenging in organizational environments that do not necessarily offer incentives, organizational designs, or technological infrastructures to facilitate collaborative behaviour. Nevertheless, Peter Gloor from MIT argues that collaborative innovation networks (COINs) "are the best engines to drive innovation."[72]

Increased connectivity between all elements within the system can serve to enhance the organization's adaptive potential through accelerated knowledge creation and learning. The Connective orientation captures the degree to which networks and information technology are used effectively to enhance data, information, and knowledge sharing within and between organizational levels, functions, and virtual communities.

Some key questions for you to ask yourself related to your organization's *Connective* Orientation

- To what extent do we foster cross-functional communication?
- To what extent do we leverage technology to accelerate idea and knowledge sharing?

- To what extent do we reach out and connect with a diversity of people and networks to stimulate innovative thinking?

Lessons from the Research Field – Collaborative and Connective Orientations

Applying the OGI within organizations, leaders indicated:

A. Without the strategic will to enhance its Connective capacity, organizations may be diluting an inherent advantage that they possess as large organizations — their economies of scale.

B. Results indicated that the Connective Orientation was among the lowest scoring dimensions. Organizations need to take the importance of creating enabling technological platforms more seriously if they wish to elevate their firm's overall ability to innovate and compete successfully in the new era of hyper-accelerated technological advancements.

C. There was a belief that if the organization was more effective at collaboratively pooling resources from each of the business units and maintained a more focused innovation strategy, the organization as a whole would be much more effective at innovation.

D. Results indicated that while Collaboration is critically important, organizations require a structure that enables and encourages the cross-pollination of ideas and knowledge across the organization. This will help to break down ingrained functional and professional assumptions and create the potential for new innovative ideas to emerge due to the exchange between organizational members.

The ALIGN Mindset supports the *Leadership* and *Cultural* Orientations

- Integrating values, mission, vision, and strategies
- Engaging the hearts and minds of people
- Encouraging responsible risk-taking

7. Leadership Orientation

There is no innovation without leadership support.
- Inconvenient Truth #9

It is difficult to overemphasize the importance of leadership. Aside from countless publications espousing the importance of leadership, drawing on my own experience and research with organizations I contend that any innovation agenda is doomed to failure without meaningful support from the CEO and the executive team. I would go further by saying it isn't enough to have their support, they must also be effective at *leading* innovation, which requires unique mindsets and skillsets that do not always come naturally to them.

First and foremost, leaders are responsible for setting the strategic direction of the organization, and the firm's innovation strategy must be seen and communicated as an integral component of the organization's ability to win over the long run. Leaders strongly influence organizational effectiveness through the way in which they shape organizational strategies, ensuring they in fact select the right kinds of innovations that will lead to sustained organizational vitality.

Without the appropriate strategic alignment and commitment, it is difficult for managers and leaders of innovation to acquire and indeed retain the resources required to see the innovations through. Case in point, in one of the organizations I was conducting research in, managers faced a chronic, yearly pattern of being asked to redirect money they were given to support innovation efforts to other, more pressing, short-term financial targets, which Govindarajan and Trimble describe as the "performance engine."[73]

While this organization intellectually knew the benefits of innovation, they did not have the right cultural mindset — driven by an unwillingness or inability of the senior leadership — to effectively support mid- to long-term innovation efforts. Managers articulated frustration with this pattern as they believed there to be a real need to innovate, although in actuality, the organization's environment did not support it.

The CEO and senior executives ultimately have the power to influence not only *where* the organization ought to go by way of its strategy, but also *how* it will achieve that strategy and *by what means* it will execute it. Given that innovation is, as I suggest, a *whole system phenomenon,* it needs to be properly integrated into the organization's broader business strategy because it demands the money, time, attention, skillsets, and commitment from multiple functions across the organization to make it happen effectively.

Collectively, the leadership envisions, promotes, and supports the core strategies believed to drive future success for the organization, and in turn allocates resources weighted according to their perceived relevance and impact. Senior leaders and their managers also reinforce, through their actions and decisions, the degree to which innovation is valued and supported.

The Leadership Orientation assesses the extent to which leaders and managers formulate and enact strategies and behaviours that positively support an organization's ability to successfully innovate and grow.

Some key questions for you to ask yourself related to your organization's Leadership Orientation

- To what extent does the leadership enhance motivation and commitment in support of innovation?
- To what extent does the leadership align corporate values, strategy, vison, and mission with the innovation and/or transformation agenda?
- To what extent does the leadership meaningfully promote candor, trust, and responsible risk-taking across the organization?

8. Cultural Orientation

In Chapter 4, I shared a model labelled, "Elements of the Organization's Environment," which made distinctions between an organization's climate, culture, and mindset. Culture runs deep within organizations given it represents underlying values, assumptions, and beliefs generated and reinforced over time related to how things "ought to be"

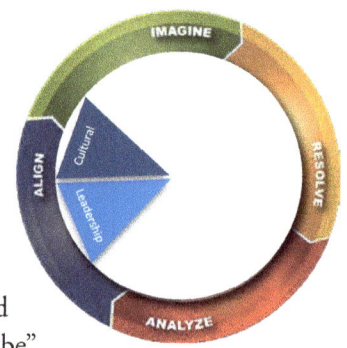

and how they ought to get done in order to achieve effective results. As such, culture is much more stable and thus harder to change than people's transitory attitudes or levels of engagement at a particular moment in time.

While an organization's culture may be stable, it does not mean that it is static. Quite the contrary. An organization's culture is a dynamic, active force that influences organizational *sensemaking*.[74] Or to put it another way, culture influences how leaders and employees go about "making sense" of what actually occurs within the organization. For example, how leaders act and interact with others, how decisions get made, what kinds of thinking and behaviour are valued and reinforced, and what are not. Culture, then, not only influences how people think, it touches them emotionally and guides individual and collective action across the organization.

There is no shortage of research related to how culture impacts organizations. In their book, *Complexity and the Nexus of Leadership*,[75] Goldstein, Hazy, and Lichtenstein explore the notion of "attractors," which operate within open adaptive systems, such as organizations. Like corporate culture, attractors influence employee behaviour. They suggest that "every organization's business model — including the routines that get the work done, and the dominant logic that makes sense of the whole process — forms an attractor that draws forth a certain kind of behavior from everyone in the company to maintain a level of stability."

Most importantly, the behaviours that are precipitated by these attractors are largely "driven by implicit rather than explicit forces that tend to be tacit and not necessarily easy to surface." Underlying, tacit forces such as "attractors" and "shared mental models" have been shown to meaningfully influence and shape organizational behaviour and, as such, may illuminate certain aspects of an organization's culture.

In *Corporate Culture and Performance*, John Kotter and James Heskett suggest that corporate culture shapes the behaviour of the firm's management to the same degree as "formal structures, systems, plans, and policies."[76] It is suggested here that culture can be described as a largely implicit, affectively loaded, organizational phenomenon that emerges when leaders, managers, and employees are thrown into situations that demand decisions and effective action such as coping with corporate and environmental change or being called upon to innovate and modify current practices.

In her research, Harvard professor, Theresa Amabile found that an organization's environment has a mediating effect on innovation. Amabile suggests "the work environment can exert a powerful impact on creativity by influencing motivation."[77] According to her componential model of creativity, the environment primarily influences "task motivation" and "creativity skills," which in turn directly influence an organization's ability to innovate. When attempting to assess an organization's ability to grow, it is important to capture the way in which the organization's culture is supporting or constraining its innovation efforts.

An organization's culture consists of various dimensions such as espoused values that guide individual and collective action, as well as mindsets and implicit assumptions used by leaders, managers, and key contributors while engaging in problem solving and decision making. The Cultural Orientation attempts to capture the degree to which the organization's culture motivates and encourages members of the organization to engage in innovative thinking and behaviour.

Some key questions for you to ask yourself related to your organization's Cultural Orientation

- What is the level of trust between leaders, managers, and employees?
- To what extent does the organizational environment support innovation and growth?
- What is the level of employee engagement within your organization?

Lessons from the Research Field – Leadership and *Cultural Orientations*

Applying the OGI within organizations, leaders indicated:

A. The organization's culture and leadership strongly shape an organizational environment that is conducive to nurturing and executing innovation.

B. Results indicated that there can be confusion concerning where and how innovation might participate in supporting the organization's efforts at being more competitive without a clearly articulated innovation strategy by the leadership.

C. An interesting finding pertained to the relationship that exists between organizational effectiveness and innovation. Importantly, that relationship can create either a vicious or a virtuous cycle. In short, if the organization is not effective at innovating, it may in fact worsen the overall effectiveness of the organization. As organizational effectiveness decreases, the perceived need for innovation increases. Yet, if the organization is not disciplined in the introduction and execution of innovation, attempts at innovation may stall or worse fail, creating more frustration and disengagement among organizational members, not to mention ineffective utilization of precious resources.

D. Innovation reflects a level of vitality within an organization. There may be an interesting connection between an organization's ability to innovate and the level of attractiveness the organization possesses for top talent seeking employment. Top talent typically wants to be a part of a growing, vibrant, innovative company.

We have explored each of the elements on The Transformation Wheel and explored some key research findings from the field related to each of the 8 Orientations. It is now time to explore more detailed applications of the OGI (Organizational Growth Indicator), particularly related to how the OGI scores relate to an organization's actual revenue performance.

Chapter 5 References

55. World Economic Forum (2016). "The future of jobs: Employment, skills and workforce strategy for the fourth industrial revolution". www.weforum.org/reports/the-future-of-jobs (accessed on February 16, 2016)

56. The Global CEO Study. (2010). "Capitalizing on Complexity." IBM Institute for Business Value and IBM Strategy & Change, IBM.

57. Amabile, Theresa., Regina Conti, H. Coon, J. Lazenby, and Michael J. Herron. "Assessing the work environment for creativity." *Academy of Management Journal*, 39(5), 1996: 1154-1184.

58. De Geus, Arie. (1997). *The Living Company: Habits for Survival in a Turbulent Business Environment*. Boston, MA: Longview.

59. Kim, W. Chan, and Renee Mauborgne. *Blue Ocean Strategy: How to Create Uncontested Market Space and Make the Competition Irrelevant*. Boston, MA: Harvard Business Review Press, 2005.

60. The Conference Board, CEO Challenge. Research Report: "Creating Opportunity Out of Adversity: Building Innovative, People-Driven Organizations." Revised February 11, 2015.

61. Martin, Roger. (2009). *The Design of Business: Why Design Thinking Is the Next Competitive Advantage*. Boston, MA: Harvard Business Press: 37.

62. Pfeffer, Jeffrey. (2007). *What Were They Thinking: Unconventional wisdom about Management*. Boston, MA: Harvard Business School Press.

63. Brown, John Seely, and Paul Duguid. "Organizational learning and communities of practice: Toward a united view of working, learning and innovation." *Organization Science*, 2(1), 1991: 40-57.

64. March, James. "Exploration and exploitation in organizational learning." *Organization Science*, 2 (1), 1991: 71-87.

65. Senge, Peter. *The Fifth Discipline: The Art & Practice of the Learning Organization*. New York, NY: Doubleday/Currency, 1990.

66. IBM Global Technology Services: "The Toxic Terabyte: How data-dumping threatens corporate efficiency," 2006.

67. Conference Board of Canada. (2010, November). *Innovation catalysts and accelerators*. (Report). Ottawa, ON: Joseph Haimowitz & Daniel Munro.

68. Chesbrough, Henry. (2006a). Open innovation: A new paradigm for understanding industrial innovation. In H. Chesbrough, W. Vanhaverbeke, and J. West (Eds.), *Open innovation: Researching a New Paradigm*. New York, NY: Oxford University Press, 2006a: 1-12.

69. Johnson, Steven. *Where Good Ideas Come From: The Natural History of Innovation.* New York, NY: Riverhead Books, 2010: 220, 228.

70. Friedman, Thomas L. *The World is Flat: A Brief History of the Twenty-first Century.* New York, NY: Farrar, Straus & Giroux, 2005: 176.

71. Castells, Manuel. *The Rise of the Network Xociety.* 2nd ed. West Sussex, UK: Wiley-Blackwell, 2010.

72. Gloor, Peter A. *Swarm Creativity: Competitive Advantage through Collaborative Innovation Networks.* New York, NY: Oxford University Press, 2006: 17.

73. Govindarajan, Vijay and Chris Trimble. *The Other Side of Innovation: Solving the Execution Challenge.* Boston, MA: Harvard Business Review Press. 2010: 11.

74. Weick, Karl E. (1995). *Sensemaking in Organizations.* Thousand Oaks, CA: Sage Publications.

75. Goldstein, Jeffrey A., James K. Hazy and Benjamin B. Lichtenstein. *Complexity and the Nexus of Leadership.* New York, NY: Palgrave Macmillan, 2010: 58, 59.

76. Kotter, John, and James Heskett. *Corporate Culture and Performance.* New York, NY: The Free Press, 1992: 6.

77. Amabile, Theresa. *Creativity in Context: Update to the Social Psychology of Creativity.* Boulder, CO: Westview Press, 1996: 7.

CHAPTER 6

Measuring Shifts in Organizational Mindsets

"Only one in four senior managers report that training was critical to business outcomes."[78]
– Harvard Business Review, 2016

The New Organizational Performance Equation

In the Preface to this book, I introduced what I believe to be a more effective organizational performance equation, essentially putting the organization back into the equation.

> Organizational System + Leaders + Training =
> Improved Organizational Performance

In actuality, this equation can be further expanded to include measurement and evaluation, and when it does so, it can be codified as a *Virtuous Cycle*: positively evolving the organization's ability to innovate and transform adaptively over time.

Figure 7: Organizational Performance Improvement Process

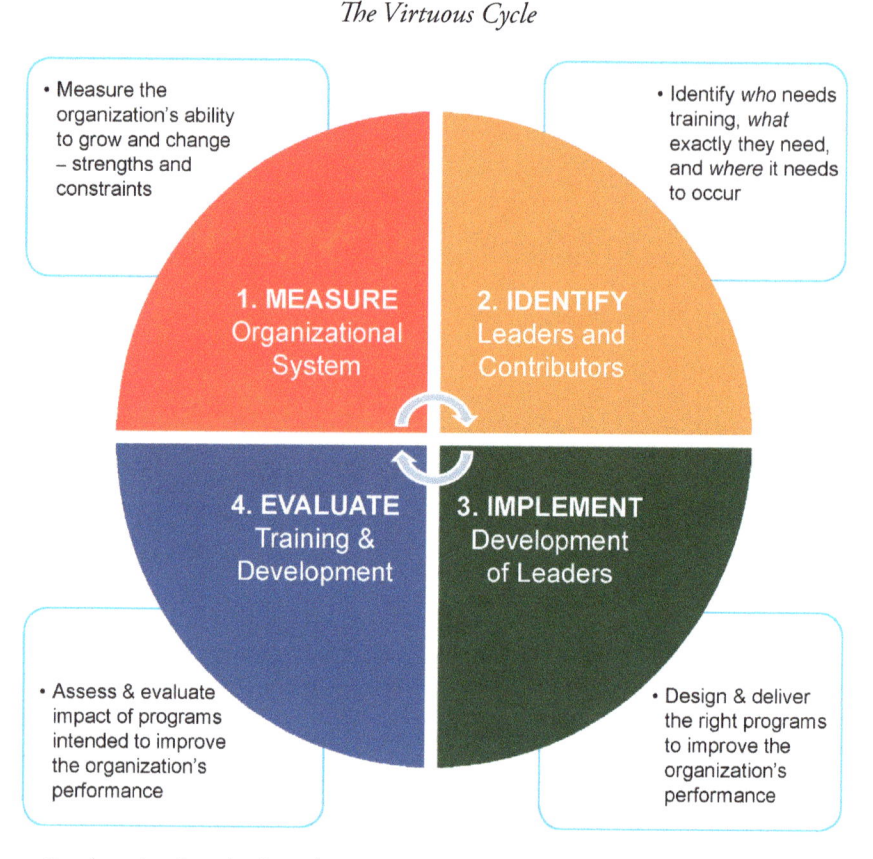

The Virtuous Cycle

- Measure the organization's ability to grow and change – strengths and constraints

1. MEASURE Organizational System

- Identify *who* needs training, *what* exactly they need, and *where* it needs to occur

2. IDENTIFY Leaders and Contributors

4. EVALUATE Training & Development

3. IMPLEMENT Development of Leaders

- Assess & evaluate impact of programs intended to improve the organization's performance

- Design & deliver the right programs to improve the organization's performance

On the other hand, when the organization is removed from the organizational performance equation, attempts to improve organizational performance by way of leadership training programs alone may lead to a *Vicious Cycle* eroding the organization's adaptive capability. This can happen when the executive team becomes frustrated with the chronic lack of results (ROI) of the training dollars invested with respect to generating growth or improving the bottom line. On the flip side, leaders who participate in the training program also get frustrated when the organization's environment, which includes its climate, culture and mindset, are not supportive or ready for shifts in thinking and behaviour promoted in the leadership development program.

As a result of this shared frustration for both the executive team and the leaders who participate in the training, organizational motivation to improve performance via training (no matter how good it might be) declines. As organizational motivation for learning declines, the organization gets caught in a *learning trap* creating a downward spiral or vicious cycle that over time may constrain its ability to adapt and respond to disruption in its environment.

Inconvenient Truth #11
Effective organizations are most likely to be successful with innovation and yet it's the ineffective organizations that need it most and who often experience numerous failed innovation attempts, a.k.a. the vicious cycle.

At a high level, the OGI is a tool to accelerate organizational learning and as such it is intended to help organizations avoid the *learning trap*. In today's environment where knowledge and technological advancements are growing exponentially, an increased capacity to learn is essential. Organizations need to find ways to learn faster and more effectively. Let's take a look at some organizations "that have used" the OGI to support their growth and transformation efforts. To preserve confidentiality, all of the actual names of the organizations shared in the following case examples are identified only by their organizational type.

The College

The College is a post-secondary academic institution strongly focused on advancing skills in creativity and innovation, and is very interested in learning more about its overall innovative potential as an academic institution. In 2013, The College was in the throws of initiating their transformational journey in becoming a more creatively focused institution, so they were also interested in their institution's "readiness" for change.

In a very meaningful and literal way, The College embodied the process identified in the *Organizational Performance Improvement Process – Virtuous Cycle* model depicted in Figure 7. In other words, Step One: they began with utilizing the OGI diagnostic tool to understand their organizational system's current state of "readiness" for innovation and organizational change. From there, Step Two: leveraging the OGI, they were able to identify specific leadership levels and functions within the organization that, if left unaddressed, would constrain their transformation efforts. It also reinforced the need to focus on developing creativity and innovation, given the OGI clearly demonstrated that the organization's current cultural mindset was not supporting their "strategic" desire to advance creative and innovative thinking as an institution.

Coincidentally, anticipating their need to elevate creative and innovative thinking skills among administrators and faculty, The College set out to deliver training programs to boost skills in deliberate creativity, specifically, creative problem solving (CPS). As such, Step 3 was initiated through the implementation of CPS, which aligned with their OGI results, indicating a clear need for the skills developed within CPS.

The College re-administered the OGI in 2015, thereby initiating Steps 3 and 4 of the Organizational Performance Improvement Process. The OGI provided two levels of evaluation for The College.

- First, it allowed them to measure the extent to which their organization had positively strengthened its creative mindset overall.

- Second, given the OGI allows for up to ten custom questions to be used during the second administration, The College was able to evaluate the impact of the CPS training they conducted. In other words, was there a difference in OGI scores for those that had completed CPS training versus those that had not.

As we'll see in their actual results, The College was able to use the OGI metrics to further refine and extend their training and organizational development initiatives going forward beyond 2015. At the time of this writing, they are planning for a third administration, thereby continuing the virtuous cycle of organizational performance improvement.

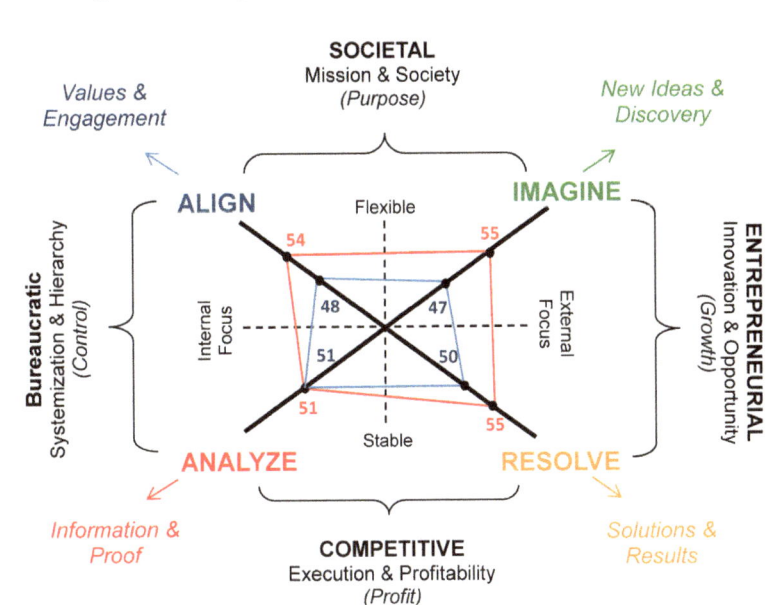

The College: 4 Principal Mindsets Compared (2013 and 2015)

SOCIETAL — Mission & Society (Purpose)
COMPETITIVE — Execution & Profitability (Profit)
Bureaucratic — Systemization & Hierarchy (Control)
ENTREPRENEURIAL — Innovation & Opportunity (Growth)

- ALIGN — Values & Engagement
- IMAGINE — New Ideas & Discovery
- ANALYZE — Information & Proof
- RESOLVE — Solutions & Results

Axes: Flexible / Stable, Internal Focus / External Focus

Scores (2013 / 2015):
- ALIGN: 48 / 54
- IMAGINE: 47 / 55
- ANALYZE: 51 / 51
- RESOLVE: 50 / 55

The College – 2013 ─────
The College – 2015 ─────

Within a sixteen-month timeframe, The College achieved a meaningful shift in its cultural mindset. Specifically, it shifted positively in the direction aligned with its strategic mandate to strengthen its creative and innovative capability. In 2013, the IMAGINE Mindset scored a 47% on the OGI, placing it in Tier 2 on the Scoring Index, indicating a "marginal" ability to innovate, and its change readiness as "developing" or moderate. In 2015 the IMAGINE Mindset increased by 8 percentage points to 55 percent, putting it in a high Tier 3 position on the OGI Scoring Index, and indicating the highest positive shift in mindset, overall. This significant shift in the IMAGINE Mindset indicated that organizational members now perceived and experienced the organization as being more supportive and receptive to the generation and discovery of new ideas, which is a fundamental ingredient of the IMAGINE Mindset.

A significant shift was also achieved with the RESOLVE Mindset indicating that not only is the organization's environment more open to new ideas, but is also more solution-focused and proficient at transforming creative ideas into tangible actions. This is the hallmark of the Entrepreneurial type of organization (IMAGINE + RESOLVE) that actively seeks to find new opportunities for growth and strives to generate creative solutions to any challenges and obstacles it encounters along the way. In this type of organization, there is a blend of creative thinking and pragmatic problem solving to find workable solutions in order to achieve effective results.

A meaningful shift was also achieved with the ALIGN Mindset, indicating the focused efforts that were undertaken by the senior leadership between 2013 and 2015 to unify the organization around a shared, transformational strategic vision were starting to take hold. For example, The College embraced a Creative Campus strategy and commitment woven into the very fabric of the institution, integrating a creative mindset and innovative thinking across scholarly disciplines and programs.

Interestingly, no change was observed in the ANALYTICAL Mindset. It was the highest scoring mindset in 2013, which made sense, theoretically, given The College is in fact an academic institution typically focused on the acquisition and dissemination of knowledge and evidence-based skills and approaches. A mindset conditioned to seeking tangible facts, information, and proof can impede the receptivity to new ideas that may fall outside of tried and true practices. Without an intentional, disciplined approach to evolving other Mindsets, the organization may remain ensconced in its habitual, if not preferred, cognitive stylistic tendencies.

The College: 4 Principal Mindsets + The 8 Orientations Compared (2013 and 2015)

	8 Orientations								4 Principal Mindsets				
	Overall	Strategic	Innovative	Learning	Collaborative	Connective	Cultural	Leadership	Creative	Imagine	Resolve	Analyze	Align	n =
Overall 2015	54	56	54	52	56	52	52	54	54	55	55	51	54	95
Overall 2013	49	51	50	48	53	48	49	52	48	47	50	51	48	77
% Difference 2015	+5	+5	+4	+4	+3	+4	+3	+2	+6	+8	+5	-	+6	

OGI SCORING TABLE
Overall -%   CLASSIFICATION / DESCRIPTION

66-100%	EXCELLING – Advanced ability to grow. Excel through change.
57-65%	THRIVING – Proficient ability to grow. Thriving through change.
48-56%	PERFORMING – Moderate ability to grow. Adaptive to change.
39-47%	DEVELOPING – Marginal ability to grow. Moderately adaptive to change.
≤38%	LAGGING – Low ability to grow. Low adaptability to change.

The OGI provides a total Overall Score for your company, as well as scores related to the 8 Orientations and 4 Principal Mindsets. For The College, the overall score in 2013 was 49% putting it at the low end of Tier 3. Overall, it increased 5 percentage points to 54 percent in 2015 moving it to the high end of Tier 3. This represents a meaningful shift in just 16 months. It also speaks to an important point. The OGI Scoring Index indicates where the company is right now and helps to level set senior leadership's expectations related to how fast an organization can reach higher Tiers on the Index.

In my experience, it is perfectly reasonable and achievable (with attention and effort) for an organization's total Overall Score to rise from a low Tier 3 to a high Tier 3 within sixteen months. On the other hand, it would be unrealistic to think that an organization could shift from a Tier 2 to a Tier 4 for example, in just sixteen months. The good news is that organizations can track their progress — quantitatively — year over year.

Looking at the 8 Orientation scores for The College, we can see that the Creative Orientation increased the most, by 6 percentage points. This was a welcome finding given their transformational vision to nurture and embed creativity into the DNA of their institution. The Strategic Orientation increased by 5 percentage points, which also demonstrated that their vision to be more creative and innovative was now better integrated into The College's broader operational and strategic mandate.

The greatest gains were seen in the Creative Orientation and the IMAGINE Mindset, which is primarily where they were most interested in seeing improvement. A key question was, "What occurred within the institution over the sixteen months to generate meaningful improvements in their OGI scores?" This takes us to the "evaluation" phase of the Organizational Performance Improvement Process, leveraging the OGI.

Evaluating Training Impact

In collaboration with the International Centre for Studies in Creativity at Buffalo State, The College initiated an intensive commitment to initiate the development of creative thinking, and problem solving skills (CPS) for faculty and administrators across the institution. Looking at the following table, we can see that ninety-five administrators and faculty members completed the OGI assessment in 2015. Several customized questions were asked, notably, "Did you participate in the CPS training? Yes or No." As you can see, fifty-eight of the OGI respondents had completed the CPS training and thirty-seven had not yet had the opportunity to do so. Most importantly, the differences in the OGI scores between the two groups was significant.

With the OGI, an organization can assess the extent to which an organization's training programs designed to improve its innovative and transformative capability are actually making an impact or not. Further, are the training programs making an impact in theoretically aligned areas, for example, is "creativity training" improving the Creative Orientation on the OGI?

The College: CPS Training – Those Who Participated Compared to Those Who Did Not

	8 Orientations								4 Principal Mindsets				
	Overall	Strategic	Innovative	Learning	Collaborative	Connective	Cultural	Leadership	Creative	Imagine	Resolve	Analyze	Align	n =
Overall 2015	54	56	54	52	56	52	52	54	54	55	55	51	54	95
Overall 2013	49	51	50	48	53	48	49	52	48	47	50	51	48	77
YES	56	59	57	53	59	55	55	57	57	58	57	52	57	58
NO	50	52	50	50	52	47	47	50	48	51	52	49	50	37
% Difference 2015	+6	+7	+7	+3	+7	+8	+8	+7	+9	+7	+5	+3	+7	

OGI SCORING TABLE
Overall -% CLASSIFICATION / DESCRIPTION

66-100% EXCELLING – Advanced ability to grow. Excel through change.
57-65% THRIVING – Proficient ability to grow. Thriving through change.
48-56% PERFORMING – Moderate ability to grow. Adaptive to change.
39-47% DEVELOPING – Marginal ability to grow. Moderately adaptive to change.
≤38% LAGGING – Low ability to grow. Low adaptability to change.

The OGI results indicate that the CPS training not only had a significant impact overall, but in theoretically aligned areas within the OGI as well. The findings demonstrated statistically significant differences in several areas, most notably the Creative and Innovative Orientations and the IMAGINE Mindset, each of which tap into the skills being taught in CPS. Those individuals who participated in the CPS program had a considerably more favourable perception of The College's creative and innovative capability. Given the positive impact of the CPS training, the senior executives of The College were no doubt pleased with the results and were able to justify continued investment in CPS training going forward.

When developing the OGI, I was intent on creating a tool that could be used across various industries and sectors given that all organizations cannot escape the need to enhance their growth and change agility. The College case study indicates that the OGI can be used to support positive growth and transformation in academic settings. Let's now explore its application in a mid-sized, family-operated, commercially-focused company.

Chapter 6 References

78. Beer, Michael, Magnus Finnstrom and Derek Schrader. "Why Leadership Training Fails – and What to Do About It," *Harvard Business Review*, October 2016.

CHAPTER 7

Measuring Shifts in an Organization's Growth Mindset

Education and Food Service Sector

A company in the Education and Food Service sector, we'll call it EduFood, is a mid-sized, family-run enterprise that provides both educational and food services for children. The CEO has a vision for growth and wants to ensure his organization has the "transformational readiness" it requires to achieve his growth mandate. The CEO implemented the OGI in 2014 to attain a baseline measure of the organization's ability to grow through new value creation and adaptive transformation. EduFood re-administered the OGI in 2015 and again in 2017 to quantitatively track improvements in its growth and adaptive capabilities, as well as the training and organizational development initiatives it implemented along the way to achieve its growth mandate.

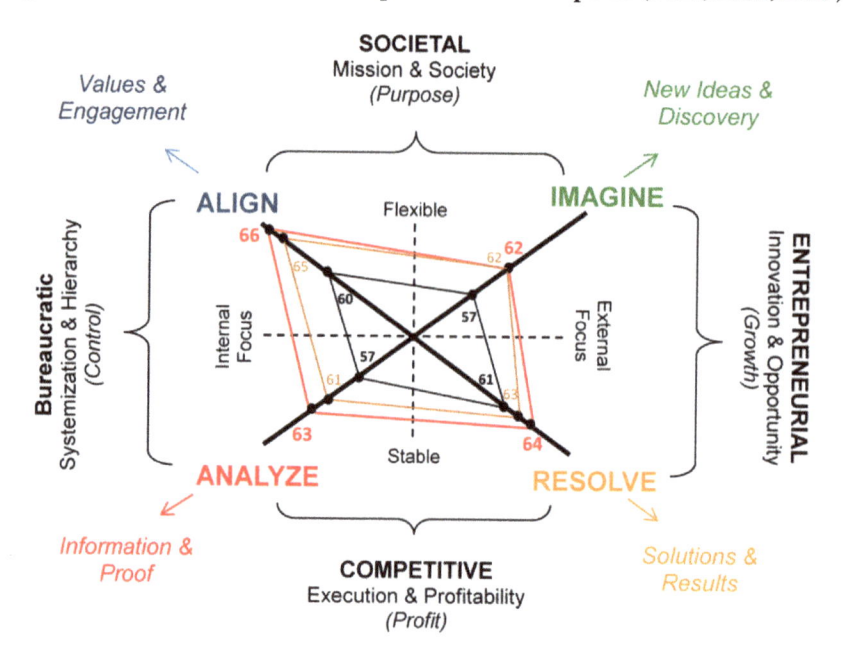

Figure 8: EduFood Overall: 4 Principal Mindsets Compared (2014, 2015, 2017)

Values & Engagement

SOCIETAL
Mission & Society
(Purpose)

New Ideas & Discovery

Bureaucratic
Systemization & Hierarchy
(Control)

ALIGN — 66
Flexible
IMAGINE — 62
65
60
57
Internal Focus
External Focus
57
61
61
63
63
Stable
64

ANALYZE
RESOLVE

ENTREPRENEURIAL
Innovation & Opportunity
(Growth)

Information & Proof

COMPETITIVE
Execution & Profitability
(Profit)

Solutions & Results

To start, EduFood is another excellent example of an organization that is enacting the new *Organizational Performance Improvement Equation* and is benefiting from the resultant virtuous cycle of learning, growth, evaluation, and organizational improvement. Make no mistake, this kind of commitment to growth and organizational transformation cannot happen without a CEO and senior team willing to invest energy and resources required to make it happen.

EduFood's improvement over a three-year time period can be seen in Figure 8. The black-lines represent EduFood's cognitive stylist patterning — cultural mindset — in 2014. It is noteworthy to see how EduFood's overall mindset has not only increased, but it has become more balanced over the last three years, indicating an organization that is not underusing or overusing any one mindset. The more expansive and balanced an organization's cultural mindset is, the greater its ability to generate growth and transform its systems, structure, and processes as required to maximize long-term success within its market space.

In 2014, for example, the Imagine (57%) and Analyze (57%) Mindsets were less developed. Notice how the Align (60%) and Resolve (61%) Mindsets are stretched out, while the Imagine and Analyze Mindsets are pinched in.

This pattern can indicate an organization that has a strong culture and values although it may be too top-down driven, which can happen in entrepreneurial and/or family-run enterprises. While this is not necessarily a bad thing, it can constrain an organization's ability to grow without building the capability of next level leaders and empowering them to make meaningful decisions.

In response to this first level of analysis in 2014, EduFood engaged in two key initiatives: one was to develop a new organizational Charter supported by a *Values In Action* (VIA) program to create a shared sense of purpose, identity, and ways of working among leaders and staff to elevate commitment and engagement throughout the organization. The second initiative, beginning midway through 2014 consisted of the development of a comprehensive organizational development (OD) framework and *Growth Leadership Program*. This program was designed to support the development of skills, competencies, attitudes, and behaviours required to support organizational growth and transformation. The program was initiated with the senior leaders and then was introduced to their next level managers.

Looking at EduFood's cultural mindset in 2015 (the orange-coloured lines) compared to 2014, we can see there was a marked improvement in all 4 Mindsets, particularly with Align (65%), Imagine (62%), and Analyze (61%). Additionally, Figure 9 shows more detail related to the changes that were achieved in each of the 8 Orientations.

Figure 9: EduFood – The 8 Orientations + 4 Mindsets 2014 and 2015 Compared

		8 Orientations								4 Principal Mindsets				
	Overall	Strategic	Innovative	Learning	Collaborative	Connective	Cultural	Leadership	Creative	Imagine	Resolve	Analyze	Align	n =
EduFood Overall 2014	59	63	58	60	57	57	61	62	56	57	61	57	60	41
EducFood Overall 2015	63	66	60	62	61	61	67	65	64	62	63	61	65	40
% Change	+4	+3	+2	+2	+4	+4	+6	+3	+8	+5	+2	+4	+5	

OGI Score TIER Performance Rating	TIER 5 [≥ 66%]	TIER 4 [65-57%]	TIER 3 [56-48%]	TIER 2 [47-39%]	TIER 1 [≤38%]
Ability to Grow and Transform	Advanced/ Excelling	Proficient/ Thriving	Moderate/ Adapting	Marginal/ Developing	Poor/ Lagging
Potential Revenue Growth Capability (% Δ)	[≥25%]	[24-10%]	[9-1%]	[0 - -8%]	[≥ -9%]

EduFood's overall OGI scores shifted from a low Tier 4 in 2014 (59%) to a high Tier 4 (62%) in 2015, which shows meaningful improvement. High Tier 4 organizations will typically be proficient at innovating products and services, and effective at creating new value for their customers. They will also have a more *proactive* rather than a *reactive* stance to the market, which is critical in thriving through disruptive market environments. EduFood is actually comprised of four completely different businesses, each with their own, unique market challenges. In aggregate, EduFood achieved 12% growth in 2015 putting it into a low Tier 4 rating. Their Tier 4 OGI rating also positioned them to effectively manage through significant disruption in two of their businesses through 2016 and 2017.

Evaluating Training Impact

The Director of Human Resources at EduFood leveraged OGI's customized question capability to gauge the impact of their new Charter and Values in Action (VIA) program. Specifically, with the second administration of the OGI in 2015, they asked employees various questions, two of which will be cited here.

Question #1: *"Since the VIA rollout, has Charter content been consistently used in communication with you, Yes or No?"* and

Question #2: *"Since the VIA rollout, have the Charter Values been incorporated consistently into meetings, Yes or No?"*

Looking at Figure 10, the data suggests that EduFood's new Charter and VIA initiatives contributed to their meaningful increase in OGI scores between 2014 and 2015.

Figure 10: EduFood – Assessing Charter and VIA Impact 2014-2015

	8 Orientations								4 Principal Mindsets				
	Overall	Strategic	Innovative	Learning	Collaborative	Connective	Cultural	Leadership	Creative	Imagine	Resolve	Analyze	Align	n =
EduFood Overall 2015	63	66	60	62	61	61	67	65	64	62	63	61	65	40
Question #1 "YES"	64	68	62	64	63	62	68	66	65	64	65	62	66	36
Question #1 "No"	50	50	40	50	48	51	55	53	48	45	50	51	51	4
Score Δ-Yes to Question	+14	+18	+22	+14	+15	+11	+13	+12	+17	+19	+15	+11	+15	
Question #2 "YES"	64	67	61	63	61	61	68	66	64	63	64	62	65	34
Question #2 "NO"	59	59	53	60	59	61	63	60	60	55	61	58	59	6
Score Δ-Yes to Question	+5	+8	+8	+3	+2	0	+5	+6	+4	+8	+3	+4	+6	

The results indicate that the incorporation and reinforcement of the Charter and VIA concepts and tools have a considerable and positive impact on employee experience at EduFood. Aside from showing that the initiatives had a positive ROI, it also indicated the need for leaders and managers to continue to reinforce the tools and values in ongoing, daily interactions, as well as more formally in meetings. Given these positive findings, EduFood was able to justify continued investment in the program, and saw the need to continue to embed the philosophy and tools into their ways of working as an organization.

As such, in the third administration of the OGI in 2017 another question was asked that again showed a significant finding: Question: *"Have you attended a VIA orientation and/or refresher in the past 3 years, Yes or No?"*

Figure 11: EduFood – Assessing VIA Impact 2015-2017

	8 Orientations									4 Principal Mindsets				
	Overall	Strategic	Innovative	Learning	Collaborative	Connective	Cultural	Leadership	Creative	Imagine	Resolve	Analyze	Align	n =
EduFood Overall 2017	63	62	60	63	64	60	68	66	63	62	64	63	66	56
Question #1 "YES"	64	62	60	64	65	61	68	67	64	62	64	63	66	44
Question #1 "No"	62	62	62	61	62	60	65	62	59	60	64	63	65	12
Score Δ-Yes to Question	+2	0	-2	+3	+3	+1	+3	+5	+5	+2	0	0	+1	

Figure 11 results indicate that the continued reinforcement and implementation of the VIA program at EduFood has contributed to a sustained lift in OGI scores from 2015 to 2017. Furthermore, the VIA program has continued to generate in their employees more favourable workplace experiences and impressions of EduFood's growth and transformative capabilities.

In addition, the VIA program is having an impact in theoretically aligned areas within the OGI. Namely, the Cultural (+3), Leadership (+5), Collaborative (+3) and Creative (+5) Orientations, as well as the Imagine (+2) and Align (+1) Mindsets. For example, the VIA program focuses on values such as collaboration, integrity, growth, engagement, and excelling.

Lasting Impact

There were many more indicated actions that were provided to EduFood from the OGI analysis related to each of their divisions and functions. In closing, an important 2017 finding for EduFood shown in Figure 11 is that the positive shift it experienced in its overall OGI scores has been largely sustained between 2015 and 2017 indicating that the changes were deeply embedded into the cultural/environmental fabric of the organization. In other words, the cultural improvements were not superficial, temporary shifts in attitudes and perceptions.

Inconvenient Truth #12
Engagement surveys are useful, but not substantive enough to fully grasp, describe, and enable how to improve organizational innovation and transformation.

Winning a "Top Culture Award" in 2017 in their business category is a good example of the efforts they have made as an organization to evolve and grow. Notably, the Cultural (68%) and Leadership (66%) Orientations, in conjunction with the Align (66%) Mindset continue to remain as EduFood's highest OGI dimensions, which points to their unique brand identity as an organization that involves nurturing a growth mindset with all members of the organization, and expanding their reach as an organization while making a positive impact on society.

The EduFood case study indicates that the OGI is effective in mid-sized organizations, but what about large-scale organizations with affiliates in multiple countries around the world? The next chapter explores the application of the OGI in three global companies.

CHAPTER 8

Global Companies Improving Growth Capability with the OGI

In this chapter, we will review the application of the OGI in three global companies who are interested in driving growth and strengthening their innovative mindset. It will be particularly interesting to connect their real revenue growth rates with their OGI results. These case studies help to demonstrate how the OGI accurately aligns with actual performance metrics related to growth and transformation as outlined in the OGI Scoring Index.

The Anca Group – Manufacturing Sector

The Anca Group, headquartered in Melbourne, Australia, is a global manufacturer that specializes in the design and development of machine tools, motion control systems, and metal fabrication. Anca is considered a leader in its market space, known for its innovation and product superiority in both technology and software.

Despite its history of impressive performance in both growth and profitability, in April 2016, The Anca Group set out on a journey to further increase its innovative capability. The goal for Anca was to explore strategies to reshape its culture in ways that would enable continued growth through innovation, enhancing creative thinking, and innovative behaviours across the organization.

Anca administered the OGI within each of its three divisions, across fifteen countries in Asia, Southeast Asia, Australia, Europe, and North America. The objective was to attain a robust quantitative, baseline measure indicating both the strengths and potential "constraints" to growth through innovation within each of the companies and locations around the world.

Incidentally, Anca is another excellent example of an organization doing it right when it comes to executing a corporate strategy intended to improve its growth and transformative capability. That is, they are utilizing the *New Organizational Performance Equation* by starting first with "assessing the organization's ability to grow and change" through leveraging the common language, framework, and metrics provided by the OGI. At the time of this writing, the CEO indicated to me that Anca "just had a team go around the world workshopping the outcomes from the OGI as part of acting on the next steps."

a. Anca will re-administer the OGI to track and evaluate results once enough time has passed to allow for some of their performance improvement initiatives to take hold. At that time, they will be able to measure and evaluate the extent to which Anca's innovative mindset has shifted overall, as well as specifically within each of its three business units, countries and regions, and

b. the extent to which the specific training and organizational development initiatives have been successful in improving the organization's ability to grow through innovation and adaptive change.

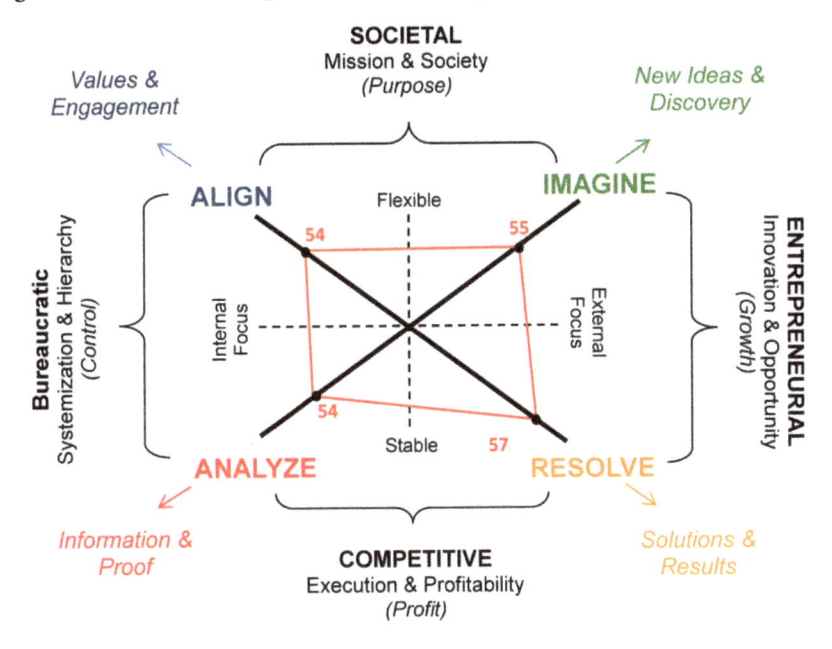

Figure 12: The Anca Group – Overall 4 Principal Mindsets 2016

```
                         SOCIETAL
                      Mission & Society
  Values &               (Purpose)          New Ideas &
  Engagement                                 Discovery
        ↖                                        ↗
            ALIGN        Flexible      IMAGINE
                    54              55
Bureaucratic                                         ENTREPRENEURIAL
Systemization                                        Innovation &
& Hierarchy      Internal          External         Opportunity
(Control)         Focus              Focus           (Growth)
                    54              57
            ANALYZE      Stable      RESOLVE
        ↙                                        ↘
  Information &                              Solutions &
  Proof                 COMPETITIVE          Results
                    Execution & Profitability
                         (Profit)
```

The Invisible Made Visible

One of the advantages of utilizing the OGI is that it brings to light hidden dynamics operating within the organizational system that may potentially undermine the organization's intended strategy and/or vision if left undetected and unaddressed. The BHAG (Big Hairy Audacious Goal) for Anca is to be the *"#1 in lifetime customer experience in every division,"* whilst continuing to grow. For Anca, it's not an either/or — growth *or* customer experience — it's both growth *and* customer experience, not just in one division, but in all divisions around the world.

Now that is a BHAG, even for an already successful company like Anca. Within that context, the OGI pointed out some key stress points in various locations, functions, leadership levels, and divisions that would potentially constrain Anca's ability to achieve its BHAG if left unaddressed. With the OGI metrics, Anca has been able to target their resources, time, and energy more effectively to strengthen their performance in support of their BHAG.

Looking at Anca's overall cultural mindset, or cognitive style, in Figure 13 we can see that it is leveraging each of the 4 Principal Mindsets commensurate with an organization that currently has a *moderate* to *proficient* ability to innovate and is adaptive to change. Keeping in mind that each of the 4 Principal Mindsets are equally important in their own right in support of growth, it is desirable to see that no one mindset is underutilized.

Remember too, that this is reflective of the aggregate mindset across all three business units and locations around the world. A wide variety of company mindsets were revealed indicating the internal cultural nuances — strengths and areas in need of development to accelerate growth — within each business unit and location, globally.

Anca's strongest Mindset is Resolve (57%), which is not uncommon for manufacturing-type organizations that are largely focused on production, execution, and finding solutions to production and delivery-related challenges. The Imagine Mindset (55%) is robust for a manufacturing-type organization, which is reflective of Anca's focus, drive, and reputation in the marketplace for developing innovative products and solutions. The Align (54%) and Analyze (54%) Mindsets indicate potential opportunities for Anca to maintain their focus and achieve success at being "being first in lifetime customer experience, while continuing to grow."

The Analyze Mindset, for example, will help enhance organizational efficiencies, deliver high quality products with fewer defects, as well as offer exceptional service levels for customers while maintaining a focus on innovation and growth. The Align Mindset will serve to strengthen organizational engagement and commitment, unifying the organization around a shared strategy and approach toward the realization of their vision, which is now firmly underway.

Figure 13: The Anca Group – The 8 Orientations + 4 Mindsets 2016

	8 Orientations								4 Principal Mindsets				
	Overall	Strategic	Innovative	Learning	Collaborative	Connective	Cultural	Leadership	Creative	Imagine	Resolve	Analyze	Align	n =
Anca Overall 2016	55	57	55	50	53	56	55	55	54	55	57	54	54	183

OGI Score TIER Performance Rating	TIER 5 [≥ 66%]	TIER 4 [65-57%]	TIER 3 [56-48%]	TIER 2 [47-39%]	TIER 1 [≤38%]
Ability to Grow and Transform	Advanced/ Excelling	Proficient/ Thriving	Moderate/ Adapting	Marginal/ Developing	Poor/ Lagging
Potential Revenue Growth Capability (% Δ)	[≥25%]	[24-10%]	[9-1%]	[0 - -8%]	[≥ -9%]

The ANCA Group achieved an impressive 20.61% annual growth in 2016 over 2015, which would typically align with an OGI Tier 4 rating, with potential growth rates between (10–24%). However, there was also significant growth in its overall core market globally between 6% and 9% depending on regional differences. Given that a rising tide lifts all boats, all companies in that sector in 2016 would have expected to realize a 6–9% growth automatically. Anca's high Tier 3 rating (55% overall score) is more reflective of its current ability to grow and transform, particularly with these market dynamics factored in.

To conclude, the OGI highlighted specific factors at play within its internal environment that would potentially constrain its ability — if left unaddressed — to be first in lifetime customer experience, while continuing to grow. Anca is well positioned for continued growth and is taking tangible steps to transform its cultural mindset to be more innovative and customer focused, ensuring continued success in the future.

The Aerospace Sector

A company in the Aerospace Sector, we'll call AeroCo, is a global company with operations in multiple countries. Given that the CEO had a strategic mandate to accelerate growth worldwide, the OGI was implemented to gather a current state analysis of the organization's ability to grow and change adaptively.

AeroCo administered the OGI within each of its divisions, departments, and leadership levels across three key countries of operation. Results of the OGI diagnostic indicated a strong connection between their OGI scores and levels of actual overall revenue performance and between business units.

Figure 14: AeroCo Overall: 4 Principal Mindsets 2015

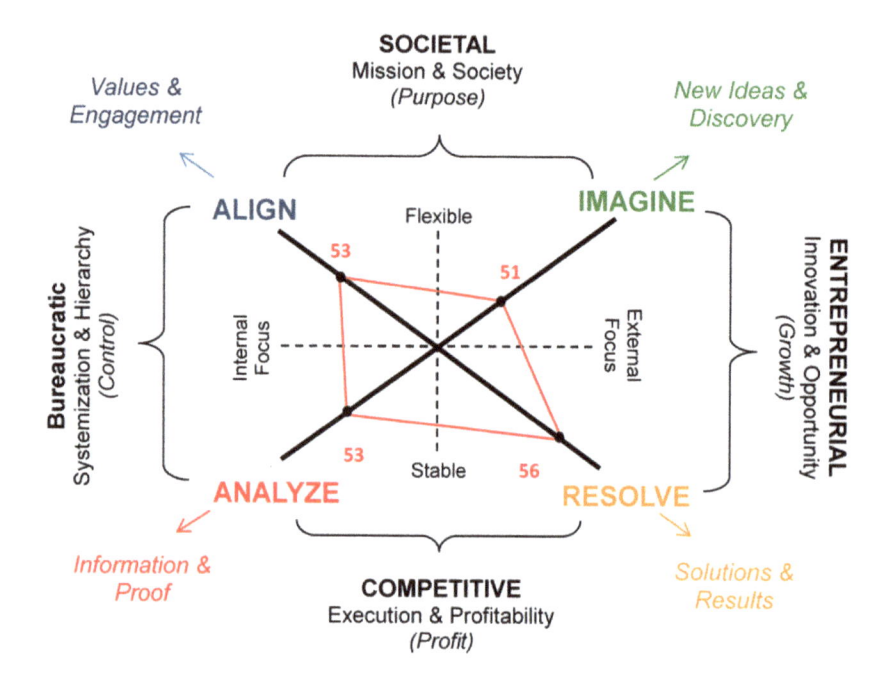

```
                         SOCIETAL
                    Mission & Society
  Values &              (Purpose)            New Ideas &
  Engagement                                  Discovery
       ↖                                         ↗
            ALIGN      Flexible      IMAGINE
                        53
                              51
  Bureaucratic    Internal          External     Entrepreneurial
  Systemization   Focus              Focus       Innovation &
  & Hierarchy                                    Opportunity
  (Control)                                      (Growth)
                        53
            ANALYZE    Stable   56  RESOLVE
       ↙                                         ↘
  Information &                              Solutions &
  Proof               COMPETITIVE              Results
                 Execution & Profitability
                         (Profit)
```

Looking at Figure 14, we can see that Resolve (56%), was AeroCo's highest scoring mindset, which indicates a cognitive emphasis on problem solving and a practical approach to resolving issues as they arise. While this is essential, if overused at the expense of the Imagine Mindset, it can develop into a more *reactive* versus a *proactive* approach to the market, which can diminish a growth focus, and potentially long-term viability. Remember, the Mindsets are reflective of where the organization focuses its attention and resources, what it deems to be relevant and important to achieve success.

Over the last decade, AeroCo has placed considerable emphasis on seeking efficiencies, implementing "Lean" and "Six Sigma" kinds of initiatives, which have proven beneficial to the bottom line. It is understandable, therefore, that this is the most developed mindset at AeroCo.

Some interesting comparisons can be made between AeroCo and The Anca Group case study. Even though they serve different markets, both companies design, engineer and manufacture specialized products globally, so some valid comparisons can be made between the two companies. First, Resolve is the highest scoring Mindset for both companies demonstrating a pattern for organizations in the Manufacturing Sector who are focused on the production and delivery of products to customers, in the most efficient way, to maximize profitability.

The Mindset of Resolve coupled with Analyze indicates an organization focused on execution and maximizing profitability, which is clearly where AeroCo has placed its emphasis over the last ten years. By comparison, Resolve coupled with Imagine indicates an organization focused on innovation and growth, and this is where The Anca Group has focused its efforts since its inception in 1974. This is clearly seen in the difference between the cognitive stylistic patterning between the two organizations, particularly with the Imagine Mindset. Notably, The Anca Group has consistently experienced revenue growth at more than double the rate of AeroCo over the last several years.

Now that is not to say that AeroCo is not successful. It is in fact a successful company although its approach to the market is different as is visually (and quantitatively) demonstrated by their OGI results and revenue growth performance. Organizations interested in maximizing efficiencies to drive profitability can afford to de-emphasize the Imagine Mindset. However, organizations interested in increasing growth cannot live without it. Table 1 below shows more interesting points of comparison.

Table 1: AeroCo – The 8 Orientations + 4 Mindsets 2015

	8 Orientations								4 Principal Mindsets				
	Overall	Strategic	Innovative	Learning	Collaborative	Connective	Cultural	Leadership	Creative	Imagine	Resolve	Analyze	Align	n =
AeroCo Overall 2015	51	53	47	48	50	51	53	55	50	51	56	53	53	115

OGI Score TIER Performance Rating	TIER 5 [≥ 66%]	TIER 4 [65-57%]	TIER 3 [56-48%]	TIER 2 [47-39%]	TIER 1 [≤38%]
Ability to Grow and Transform	Advanced/ Excelling	Proficient/ Thriving	Moderate/ Adapting	Marginal/ Developing	Poor/ Lagging
Potential Revenue Growth Capability (% Δ)	[≥25%]	[24-10%]	[9-1%]	[0 - -8%]	[≥ -9%]

AeroCo achieved 5% annual growth in 2015 after adjusting for exchange effects putting it right in line with a mid Tier 3 OGI performance rating. Their aim is to achieve double digit growth, putting it into a Tier 4 rating. This will require a meaningful increase in its Imagine Mindset, along with other key orientations within the OGI.

For example, the Innovative Orientation (47% – Tier 2) is the lowest scoring orientation, which is a significant finding for AeroCo. By comparison, The Anca Group's Innovative Orientation score was (55% – Tier 3) a full 8 percentage points higher, overall. Internally focused innovation focused on continuous improvement (e.g. Lean, Six Sigma) to remain vital support efficiency and profitability. However, given AeroCo's stated need for growth, it won't be enough. Externally focused innovation will create new value for customers through improved products and services, as well as assist at effectively responding to competitive pressures that threaten to erode AeroCo's market share.

Given the interdependencies that exist between each of the OGI Orientations, greater cross-functional collaboration and connectivity will likely serve to enhance the Learning Orientation (48% – low Tier 3), which is vital to organizational adaptation. Organizational learning enhances organizational effectiveness related to change and innovation. A greater emphasis on capturing "lessons learned" and "new knowledge" acquired through enacting change and innovation initiatives across AeroCo may help to create a virtuous cycle of knowledge creation and enhanced innovation potential.

The Strategic (53% – mid Tier 3) and Creative (50% – low Tier 3) Orientations indicate an opportunity to increase understanding and integration of the "growth agenda" (Strategic) deep and wide throughout the organization to build momentum and engagement for change and organizational transformation. Developing a cultural environment and skillset to better advance (Creative) and innovative thinking will also help AeroCo to accelerate growth.

Table 2: AeroCo – 3 Countries Compared - 2015

	Overall	8 Orientations								4 Principal Mindsets				n =
		Strategic	Innovative	Learning	Collaborative	Connective	Cultural	Leadership	Creative	Imagine	Resolve	Analyze	Align	
AeroCo Overall 2015	51	53	47	48	50	51	53	55	50	51	56	53	53	115
Country #1	52	50	47	49	50	54	52	54	50	49	55	53	53	
Country #2	58	56	53	55	55	57	62	59	59	56	61	59	59	
Country #3	51	57	45	44	48	47	48	57	48	52	52	51	51	

OGI Score TIER Performance Rating	TIER 5 [≥ 66%]	TIER 4 [65-57%]	TIER 3 [56-48%]	TIER 2 [47-39%]	TIER 1 [≤38%]
Ability to Grow and Transform	Advanced/ Excelling	Proficient/ Thriving	Moderate/ Adapting	Marginal/ Developing	Poor/ Lagging
Potential Revenue Growth Capability (% Δ)	[≥25%]	[24-10%]	[9-1%]	[0 - -8%]	[≥ -9%]

Comparing the three key countries of operation for AeroCo, we can see that Country #2 (58%) had the highest OGI scores, overall, and it did achieve the highest revenue growth (~6% after exchange effects) across the three countries of operation. Interestingly, there were significant differences of OGI scores within the four Business Units (BUs) that comprised Country #2, but the highest-performing business unit in the world in 2015 also resided in Country #2 as shown in the chart below.

Table 3: AeroCo – Country #2 – Business Unit (BU) Comparisons 2015

		8 Orientations								4 Principal Mindsets				
	Overall	Strategic	Innovative	Learning	Collaborative	Connective	Cultural	Leadership	Creative	Imagine	Resolve	Analyze	Align	n =
Country #2 Overall Score	58	56	53	55	55	57	62	59	59	56	61	59	59	
BU - A	53	50	51	54	54	53	55	55	52	54	61	59	57	
BU - B	47	41	38	47	46	47	54	47	54	46	54	53	53	
BU - C	66	67	62	62	61	68	71	69	67	62	66	63	63	
BU - D	48	49	47	44	48	39	52	51	48	51	49	51	54	

As we can see, BU – C within Country #2 achieved significantly higher OGI scores (66% overall) than the other three BUs within the same country. Most significantly, BU – C also achieved by far the highest growth rate in 2015 (~23%). Leveraging this level of analysis, organizations like AeroCo can pinpoint both the strengths and the hotspots within their organizations, whether it's at the country level, BU, functional, or leadership levels of the organization. While Country #2 is the highest-performing country overall, there are clear opportunities to further strengthen the growth and transformative capabilities within some of its BUs.

Looking at the OGI Scoring Index compared with the revenue growth rates achieved for AeroCo in 2015, we can see that the OGI scoring trend is consistent. In other words, higher OGI scores typically align with higher revenue growth rates, and lower OGI scores typically indicate lower growth rates. There is a connection between what is being identified and quantified within the organizational system's internal environment by way of the OGI and the organization's ability to grow, as evidenced by actual revenue growth performance metrics for AeroCo.

The Pharmaceutical Sector

A company in the Pharmaceutical Sector, we'll call PharmaCo, is also a global company with operations in multiple countries. Like many companies in the pharmaceutical sector, PharmaCo has an aggressive growth mandate, and it also needs to increase its change agility to adapt to increased competition, as well as ongoing changes in the regulatory environment. A key BU in PharmaCo implemented the OGI in 2016 as a way to quantitatively assess its entrepreneurial mindset and gauge the extent to which it was capable of generating increased growth over the next several years in line with the broader organization's growth objectives.

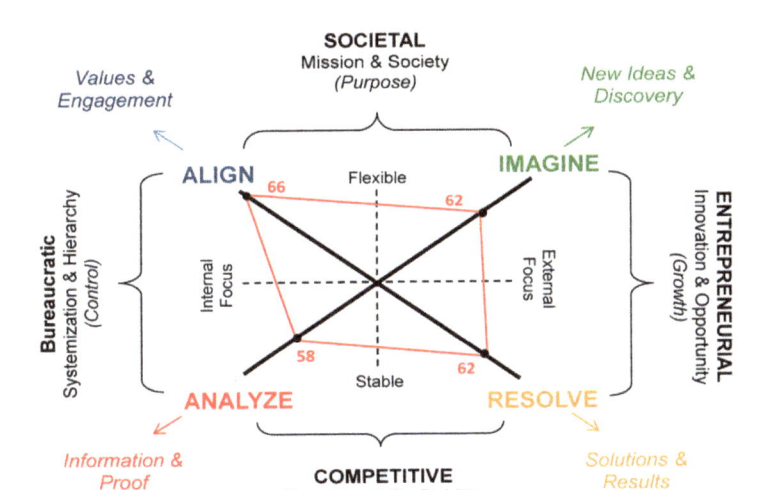

Figure 15: PharmaCo Overall: 4 Principal Mindsets 2016

```
                        SOCIETAL
                    Mission & Society
   Values &            (Purpose)          New Ideas &
  Engagement                               Discovery

            ALIGN    66              IMAGINE
                         Flexible
                                62
         Bureaucratic                      ENTREPRENEURIAL
       Systemization & Hierarchy         Innovation & Opportunity
             (Control)                          (Growth)
                  Internal              External
                   Focus                 Focus
                    58              62
                         Stable
            ANALYZE              RESOLVE

  Information &                            Solutions &
     Proof          COMPETITIVE              Results
                Execution & Profitability
                       (Profit)
```

We can see in Figure 15, that each of the 4 Principal Mindsets for PharmaCo are either in a Tier 4 or Tier 5 OGI performance rating indicating a strong, "proficient" ability to create new value through innovation, as well as an ability to not just cope with change but to "thrive" through it. The overall cognitive stylistic patterning of PharmaCo suggests it has placed considerable emphasis on building a corporate culture that is unified by shared values to guide collective action as evidenced by its high-scoring Align Mindset (66%). Importantly, those values create emotional engagement amongst employees, given they integrate benefiting society through life-changing medications with the promotion of a motivating corporate environment that promotes personal and professional growth for its employees.

The Imagine (62%) and Resolve (62%) Mindsets indicate an environment that supports new thinking and is open to finding new ways to "resolving" pressing challenges. It is an active, dynamic culture that ignites an entrepreneurial spirit in both its leaders and key contributors. This was a positive finding for PharmaCo given its desire to actively support and reinforce innovative thinking across the organization.

The Analyze (58%) Mindset, in conjunction with the other mindsets, indicates a cognitive pattern that has placed less emphasis on embedding systems and procedures that leverage data and analytics to support evidence-based decision making. This finding correlated very strongly with identified areas of opportunity for PharmaCo. It speaks to the importance of all 4 Principal Mindsets to support intelligent action related to growth and change agility.

While PharmaCo is performing extremely well, the OGI pinpointed a capability that, if improved, would drive even more effective action related to the fulfillment of their strategic objectives. For example, in addition to a growth mandate, PharmaCo is a focused on "simplification" efforts that will help to streamline processes, reduce costs, and speed up decision making. It is these kinds of efforts that require the Analyze Mindset, which is PharmaCo's lowest scoring Mindset. A healthy balance of all four Mindsets supports long-term success and viability. PharmaCo can certainly power up their Analyze Mindset, they just need to now focus more of their attention on it to achieve their simplification efforts. Their overall OGI score (62%) indicates a company that is agile and responsive to change, so changing internal practices to elevate their Analyze Mindset will likely not be problematic.

Table 4: PharmaCo – The 8 Orientations + 4 Mindsets 2016

	8 Orientations								4 Principal Mindsets				
	Overall	Strategic	Innovative	Learning	Collaborative	Connective	Cultural	Leadership	Creative	Imagine	Resolve	Analyze	Align	n =
PharmaCo Overall 2015	62	61	60	58	63	56	71	67	63	62	62	58	66	72

OGI Score TIER Performance Rating	TIER 5 [≥ 66%]	TIER 4 [65-57%]	TIER 3 [56-48%]	TIER 2 [47-39%]	TIER 1 [≤38%]
Ability to Grow and Transform	Advanced/ Excelling	Proficient/ Thriving	Moderate/ Adapting	Marginal/ Developing	Poor/ Lagging
Potential Revenue Growth Capability (% Δ)	[≥25%]	[24-10%]	[9-1%]	[0 - -8%]	[≥ -9%]

PharmaCo's overall OGI score of 62% places it in a high Tier Four performance rating. Typically, organizations with this rating could expect actual revenue growth between 18–22%. PharmaCo was tracking at 40%. However, when factoring in market growth in their product classes between 18–20%, PharmaCo is contributing approximately 20–22% growth putting it right in line with their OGI Tier 4 rating. And this is where they landed in 2016.

A more detailed view of PharmaCo's OGI results shows some interesting connections to the discussion related to their Analyze Mindset. The Connective (56%) and Learning (58%) Orientations point to clear opportunities to improve their organization's growth and adaptive capabilities. Leaders indicated that information does not flow fast enough between functions and levels (Connective), which dilutes their ability to make high-quality decisions in a timely manner.

Similarly, PharmaCo will likely improve performance by formalizing organizational "Learning" — whereby teams capture lessons learned and share best practices to accelerate and improve problem solving and decision making. The Analyze Mindset speaks, in part, to putting these kinds of organizational "learning" systems in place to increase organizational effectiveness.

Overall, PharmaCo is a highly successful company and is well positioned for continued growth through new value creation and adaptive change as evidenced by their strong OGI results.

Links to Employee Engagement

Many organizations are interested in increasing employee engagement. We have consistently found positive relationships between organizations that score high on employee engagement surveys and the Cultural, Leadership and Align dimensions on the OGI, which we saw play out with EduFood. This also demonstrates nice convergent validity between engagement surveys and related factors within the OGI.

From an OGI perspective, it acknowledges that employee engagement is crucial. However, typical engagement surveys are not designed to diagnose an organization's overall ability to grow through innovation and adaptive change. The OGI is, as we've seen demonstrated in these various case studies. Our experience to date indicates that the OGI is a tool that can augment an organization's engagement efforts by integrating them into a measure targeted at assessing its growth and transformative capability. The OGI helps to leverage investments organizations have already made in elevating their engagement by aligning them to other factors that accelerate growth and improve the bottom line.

OGI Mindsets Reflect What Organizations Do

The findings for EduFood and others reinforce the premise that an organization's cultural mindset is a reflection of where it places its attention, resources and efforts to achieve its vision, mission, and strategic intent. This is an important distinction between traditional notions of mindsets, which often take "behaviour" out of the mix. OGI Mindsets equate to *organizational enactment* — meaning they are not just a reflection of how an organization thinks or even how it feels, but are also a reflection of what the organization DOES — how it adapts and strives to fulfill its purpose and remain viable over the long term.

Links to Culture Surveys

The OGI is not just a descriptive measure of your organization's corporate culture. It is both a "descriptive" measure and an "ability" measure, and this is what helps to distinguish the OGI from other culture surveys. Yes, the OGI is "descriptive" in that it identifies an organization's cultural mindset, its unique utilization of each of the 4 Principal Mindsets as we've seen in the preceding case examples.

A purely descriptive measure would stop right there. Assessments and frameworks, which help to depict your organization's culture, serve as helpful mirrors to reflect what your culture currently is, and can indeed stimulate conversations among leaders pertaining to how your culture may need to evolve to achieve future success.

What traditional culture surveys do not do is indicate to senior leaders what the organization's current "readiness" for growth and transformation is. Nor do they typically correlate cultural descriptors to metrics such as the organization's actual revenue growth like the OGI does. The OGI, as we've seen, quantifies factors at play within the organization's internal environment that influence growth and links those outcomes to key performance indicators and results. It is in this way that the OGI is an "ability" measure, as well as a "descriptive" one.

Linking "soft" fuzzy data to "hard" performance metrics is an advantage for any organization interested in growth and improvement. But there is another perhaps less obvious advantage, which is related to managing expectations. Most CEO's want to make bold strategic moves and are typically pressured to show tangible results quickly to the Board of Directors and to shareholders. With the OGI Tier Performance Rating scale, CEOs can set more realistic goals related to the speed with which transformation can occur within their organization.

For example, it would be unrealistic for a CEO (and a Board for that matter) to expect a Tier 2 organization to shift into a Tier 4 performance rating in just one year. Further, a Tier 2 organization may not be able to absorb as much change as a Tier 4 organization would. Too much change, too fast for an organization that is not poised for growth, may lead to unintended consequences that actually undermine efforts designed to "improve" the organization. This is another reason why it's advantageous to have a diagnostic tool that is both descriptive of what the organization's culture is, and at the same time is capable of assessing the organization's ability to shift its cultural mindset to accelerate growth and change in adaptive ways.

Often, the OGI results serve to validate the gut feelings CEOs and executives have related to what their organization needs to accelerate growth. However, there are often hidden dynamics occurring that may not be in the immediate purview of the CEO.

With tangible system-wide metrics, CEO's get a more robust analysis of their organization's true capability. Further, as we've seen, the OGI helps leaders identify the right levers to pull to initiate transformation efforts, which is helpful given that leaders are not always sure where or how to kick-start their growth efforts. CEO's and executive teams also appreciate guidance around what they can do as leaders to help facilitate growth and transformation within their organizations and that will be the focus in the next chapter.

CHAPTER 9

Leadership Styles to Shift Organizational Mindsets

Which Leadership Style is Better?

So far, we have explored how the OGI assesses an organization's current capability for growth and its readiness for change leveraging 8 Orientations and 4 Principal Mindsets. Once that has been determined, the next natural questions are "So what are we going to do about it?" and "Where do we start?" And as we've seen in the preceding chapters, there are any number of "next steps" organizations can take depending on what the OGI metrics uncover.

Given the fact that an organization's leadership is integral to its success, it is important for leaders to reflect on what they can do to affect adaptive change in their organizations. Most leadership teams I've worked with are genuinely interested in finding practical ways to positively support their organization's current and future success, but they're not always clear on how to get started.

The leadership team's thinking, attitudes, and behaviours are critical when it comes to shifting organizational mindsets to be more growth-focused or adaptive. If the leadership team's *style of approach* is out of sync with the adaptive mindset required to support organizational growth and improvement, then the chances of achieving success will be reduced. The challenge is knowing what leadership styles are best for the organization given where it is now and where it believes it needs to be to achieve long-term success.

> *In short, the right style of leadership is contingent upon what is required to fulfill the organization's vision, mission, and strategic mandate.*

Each leader has their own natural style and there are, of course, many styles of leadership, each effective in certain situations and contexts. What you want to avoid is overusing, underusing, or even misusing styles of leadership that are in opposition to the kinds of thinking and behaviour required to shift the organization's mindset in adaptive ways. The trick is to enact the right style of leadership at the right time. But how do you know what's best?

In a previous chapter, I aligned the 4 Principal Mindsets to 4 Core Organizational Types. In this chapter, I will link them to 8 Common Leadership Styles. Once you've identified your organization's current growth capability and mindset leveraging the OGI metrics, you can then align unique leadership styles that are potentially most adaptive to affect positive change for your organization.

You'll notice that The Transformation Wheel, Figure 16, has been expanded to include 8 Leadership Styles that are aligned with the 4 Principal Mindsets and 8 Orientations around the wheel. Consider these as adaptive styles of leadership that are contingent upon your organization's current strengths and areas that need to be improved to strengthen your organization's ability to grow and change, adaptively.

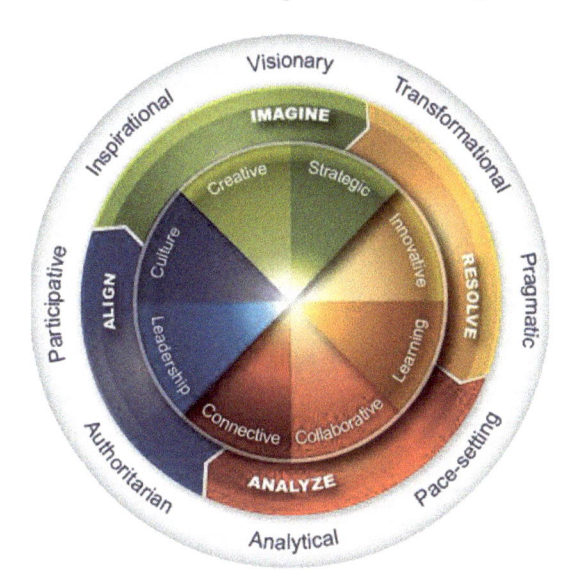

Figure 16: The Transformation Wheel Expanded with 8 Adaptive Leadership Styles

So how does it play out? Here's a quick case scenario from the field to demonstrate how it works. We administered the OGI to a mid-sized consultancy (we'll call it ConsultCo) that was interested in assessing their organization's ability to grow. The OGI results indicated that their two lowest dimensions were the Strategic and Innovative Orientations. As part of the initial high-level debrief of their results over the phone, I indicated that their senior leadership might want to adopt a more "Transformational Style" of leadership. I said this because looking at Figure 16, you can see that Transformational Style of leadership is positioned between the Imagine and Resolve Mindsets and sits directly on top of the Strategic and Innovative Orientations. This, incidentally, is the logic underlying the design of The Wheel. The Leadership Styles are positioned where they are on The Wheel because they indicate adaptive styles to support positive shifts in corresponding mindsets and orientations within The Wheel.

There was a silent pause on the phone. I asked if there was something wrong. "No, no," they said, "we cannot believe you just said that because at our senior team meeting literally two weeks ago, we decided that we needed to adopt a more Transformational Style of leadership to enhance our organization's ability to grow to achieve our strategic targets."

I believe this is to be an instructive case scenario because it speaks to the symbiotic relationship that exists between leaders and the organizational system of which the leaders are a part. This consultancy had a strategic desire to grow. Remember the combination of the Imagine and Resolve Mindsets point to an Entrepreneurial Type of organization, which focusses on innovation and growth (see Figure 17). This is exactly what "ConsultCo" was striving to be and yet there were dynamics at play within the organization, including the style of leadership being enacted by their senior leaders, that was constraining their organization's ability to grow.

In this case, ConsultCo's senior leaders had a gut feeling that they needed to shift their style of approach. The OGI metrics served to validate their hunches, but further, demonstrated the important interrelationship between their leadership style and the organization's ability to innovate and grow more successfully.

Inconvenient Truth #13
Innovation and transformation are every bit as emotional as intellectual for every member of an organization.

It makes intuitive sense that a Transformational Style of leadership would generally prove to be more adaptive to stimulate innovation and growth than say, an Authoritarian Style, which as you can see, sits directly across from or opposite to the Transformational Style on the model shown in Figure 17. Before we go any further, lets clarify the value of each of the 8 Leadership Styles in terms of how they can support more adaptive action depending on what the organization's OGI results indicate as areas needing to be strengthened.

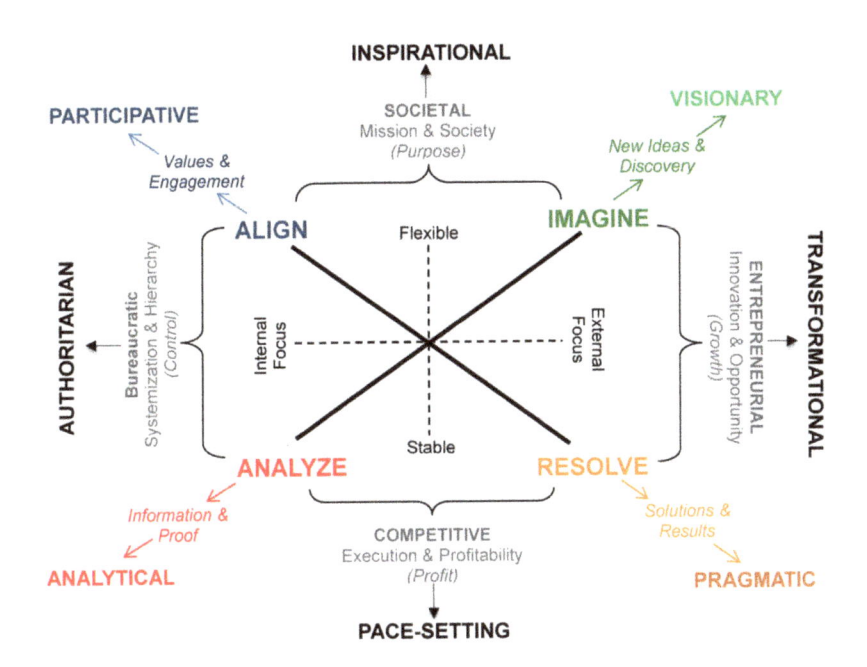

Figure 17: 8 Adaptive Leadership Styles Aligned with the 4 Principal Mindsets

```
                        INSPIRATIONAL
                              ↑
PARTICIPATIVE           SOCIETAL              VISIONARY
      ↖              Mission & Society            ↗
    Values &            (Purpose)           New Ideas &
   Engagement                                 Discovery
          ⌢⌢⌢⌢⌢⌢⌢⌢⌢⌢⌢⌢⌢⌢⌢⌢⌢
          ALIGN      Flexible      IMAGINE
                        ┆
              \         ┆         /
               \   Internal  External  /                ENTREPRENEURIAL
AUTHORITARIAN   \  Focus     Focus    /               Innovation & Opportunity  TRANSFORMATIONAL
    ←            \           /                               (Growth)                  →
   Bureaucratic   \         /
Systemization & Hierarchy
    (Control)      /       \
                  /         \
                 /    Stable  \
          ANALYZE               RESOLVE
          ⌣⌣⌣⌣⌣⌣⌣⌣⌣⌣⌣⌣⌣⌣⌣⌣⌣
    ↙                                       ↘
Information &         COMPETITIVE         Solutions &
   Proof         Execution & Profitability   Results
      ↙                (Profit)                 ↘
ANALYTICAL                                    PRAGMATIC
                              ↓
                        PACE-SETTING
```

Looking at Figure 16, you can see that the 8 Leadership Styles are related to the 4 Principal Mindsets in the same way as the 4 Organizational Types were. We began this discussion talking about the Transformational Style of leadership related to the identified needs of ConsultCo. For them, the Transformational Style of leadership was deemed to be the most adaptive style to help shift their organization's cultural mindset to be more innovative and growth focused. This finding is in line with the theoretical underpinnings of the model being shown in Figure 16.

Much has been and could be written about each of these leadership styles, however here's a brief synopsis of how I've defined and nuanced these styles, particularly as they relate to the OGI Mindsets and Organizational Types.

The Transformational Style combines the Imagine and Resolve Mindsets and is a blend of the *Visionary* and *Pragmatic* styles of leadership. Leaders who employ the Transformational Style are interested in stimulating personal and professional growth in followers, as well as growth and "transformation" for the organization as a whole. They blend a compelling vision with a grounded pragmatism that is focused on the realization of that vision. This is why it is aligned with the "Entrepreneurial" organizational type, which is focused on innovation and growth.

The Visionary Style aligns most centrally with the Imagine Mindset whose focus is on the discovery of new ideas. Leaders who employ the Visionary Style may be described as future-focused. Their energy is not so much directed on the details and planning related to the execution of their vision, rather it is on the imaginative formulation and conceptual construction of a preferred future state.

The Pragmatic Style aligns most centrally with the Resolve Mindset with its focus on solutions and results. Leaders who employ the Pragmatic Style may be described as being grounded in current reality. Their focus is not on the formulation of a vision, rather it is on the details and practical execution of a vision or objective.

The Pace-Setting Style combines the Resolve and Analyze Mindsets and is a blend of the *Pragmatic* and *Analytical* styles of leadership. Leaders who employ the Pace-setting Style are interested in efficiency and timely execution to ensure high-performance results for the organization. This is why it is aligned with the "Competitive" organizational type, which actively seeks to maximize profitability and returns for the company and its shareholders.

The Analytical Style aligns most centrally with the Analyze Mindset, which focuses on information and proof. Leaders who employ an Analytical Style could be described as utilizing a more scientific approach, leveraging objective data and logic to support evidence-based decision making. The Analytical Style values the acquisition of objective knowledge and information, and so is focused on the formulation of reliable and repeatable systems, procedures, and processes to achieve that objective.

The Authoritarian Style combines the Analyze and Align Mindsets and is a subtle blend of the *Analytical* and *Participative* styles of leadership. Leaders who employ the Authoritarian Style are focused on establishing or maintaining clear lines of "top down" decision making authority to ensure effective action and results for the organization. This is why it is aligned with the "Bureaucratic" organizational type, which is focused on hierarchy and control.

The Participative Style is connected most centrally to the Align Mindset, which focuses on values and engagement. Leaders who employ the Participative Style are more facilitative, involving followers in the formulation of goals and objectives, as well as engaging followers to participate in shared decision making.

The Inspirational Style combines the Align and Imagine Mindsets and is a blend of the *Participative* and *Visionary* styles of leadership. Leaders who employ the Inspirational Style align followers around a compelling vision and shared purpose most typically focused on the betterment of society. This is why it is aligned with the "Societal" organizational type, which focusses on a common mission and vision to improve elements of society such as impoverished groups and the environment.

As you read through the descriptions of each of these styles, you could probably identify with some more than others. You may also have recognized the dominant or most pervasive style(s) of leadership that exists within your organization. Each of these styles can be effective in certain situations and contexts, however, as we saw with ConsultCo, some may be more adaptive depending on the kind of leadership best suited to supporting your organization's current and future success.

It is instructive to refer back to some of the previous case studies to see how various Leadership Styles related to their organization's OGI results, and importantly, the style of leadership required to shift their organization's cultural mindset to support the realization of their vision and strategy.

AeroCo possesses a cultural mindset associated with a Bureaucratic–Competitive type of organization. The pervasive leadership style at the top could be described as Authoritarian, which can be adaptive in highly specialized manufacturing organizations where there is little room for error, and strict standards and quality are of utmost importance. Given that AeroCo has a growth mandate, however, overuse of the Authoritarian style of leadership may suppress involvement from the bottom up, impeding the generation of new ideas and fresh thinking required to stimulate new value creation and ways of working.

Balancing their dominant style of leadership with the thinking, attitudes, and actions associated with the Transformational Style of leadership may help to shift their organization's mindset in adaptive ways to support their strategic growth mandate. It is important to note that the Innovative Orientation was their lowest scoring OGI dimension (see Table 5) which you can also see rests directly under the Transformational Style of leadership on The Transformation Wheel showing the interrelationships that exist between the OGI Orientations, Principal Mindsets, and associated Leadership Styles.

Table 5: AeroCo – The 8 Orientations + 4 Mindsets 2015

		8 Orientations								4 Principal Mindsets				
	Overall	Strategic	Innovative	Learning	Collaborative	Connective	Cultural	Leadership	Creative	Imagine	Resolve	Analyze	Align	n =
AeroCo Overall 2015	51	53	47	48	50	51	53	55	50	51	56	53	53	115

OGI Score TIER Performance Rating	TIER 5 [≥ 66%]	TIER 4 [65-57%]	TIER 3 [56-48%]	TIER 2 [47-39%]	TIER 1 [≤38%]
Ability to Grow and Transform	Advanced/ Excelling	Proficient/ Thriving	Moderate/ Adapting	Marginal/ Developing	Poor/ Lagging
Potential Revenue Growth Capability (% Δ)	[≥25%]	[24-10%]	[9-1%]	[0 - -8%]	[≥ -9%]

The Anca Group possesses a cultural mindset associated with an Entrepreneurial type of organization. The pervasive leadership style at the top could be described as Visionary and Transformational given their rich history of product innovation in their industry. Given their organization's vision and strategic desire to be *"#1 in lifetime customer experience in every division"* while continuing to grow, it will require the inclusion of the analytical mindset and pace-setting styles of leadership to balance their Transformational Style. These styles support efficiency and timely execution associated with a competitive type of organization focused on satisfying customer needs, effectively.

Interestingly, the Collaborative and Learning Orientations were among their lowest scoring OGI dimensions and you can see it positioned near the Analytical and Pace-setting Styles of leadership on The Transformation Wheel. Notably, a team charged with meeting teams around the globe in support of progressing their cultural journey consistently heard themes among their managers related to improved communication within sites and between staff, workload planning, and product quality, to name a few examples. Each of which would benefit, in part, with a more analytical mindset and style of leadership.

PharmaCo possesses a cultural mindset associated with a Societal–Entrepreneurial type of organization. The pervasive leadership style at the top could be described as Inspirational, given its blend of a participative approach focused on building employee engagement and a visionary approach designed to coalesce the organization around an inspiring, shared vision. While this style of leadership can be supportive of growth and transformation, it may not be enough if not balanced with the Analyze mindset.

Their OGI results indicated just that. In other words, the leadership realized that they needed to enhance their Analytical and Pace-setting Styles of leadership to simplify processes in order to reduce the amount of re-work taking place, while at the same time streamlining decision-making flows. They believed these activities would help to support increased organizational agility and speed so as to be more responsive to competitive and regulatory pressures.

Interestingly, the Analyze Mindset and Connective Orientation situated near the Analytical leadership style on the Transformation Wheel were among their lowest scoring OGI dimensions, demonstrating once again the interesting interrelationships that exist for organizations related to the OGI dimensions and associated leadership styles.

The System is the People, the People are the System

As we have seen, leaders play an integral role in an organization's success. Leaders can proactively shape an organization's cultural mindset and they are also influenced by it. It is important to understand the necessary and essential interplay that occurs between leaders and the organizational systems of which they are an integral part. Much of this important "relational interplay" between, people, leaders, and the system of which they are a part is acted out implicitly each and every day throughout the organization — the implications of which can be missed without the right lens to view them.

With the OGI diagnostic, leaders can now visualize, quantitatively, the implications of these often implicit interactions that influence an organization's actions and, ultimately, its ability to grow and prosper. As we have seen, an organization's ability to grow through new value creation and adaptive change can now be measured in a practical way with the OGI. The primary objective of the tool being to support leaders in their efforts to make wiser choices as they strive to develop vibrant organizations that are better positioned for long-term success, capable of thriving, growing, and sustaining through disruption.

I invite you to think about how ready your organization is to grow through disruption and where your organization needs to shift its mindset to accelerate growth and transformation.

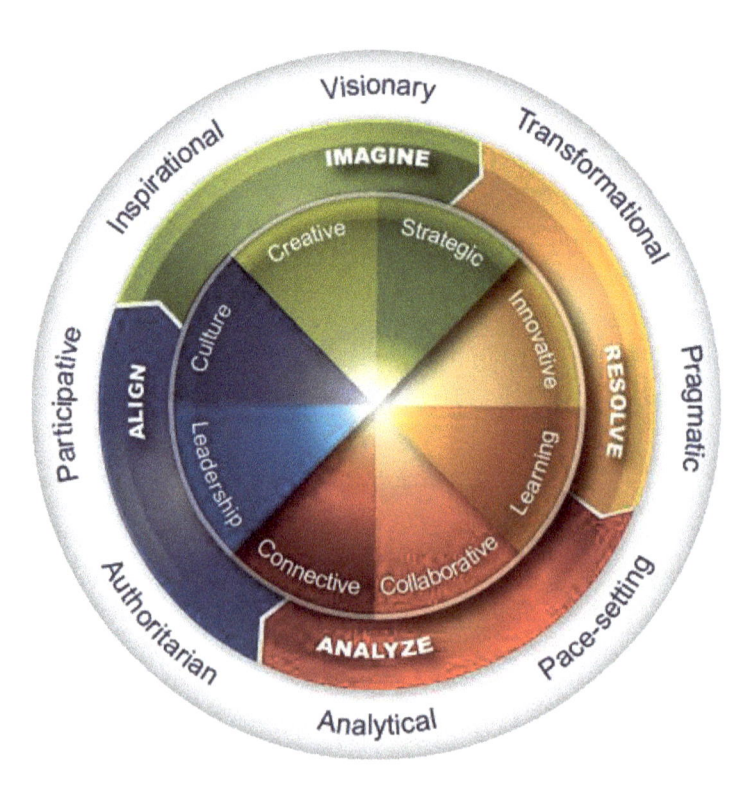

CHAPTER 10

Getting Started with the OGI

We have explored OGI applications in various sized organizations ranging from a mid-sized, family-run enterprise to large scale, global organizations, as well as from various sectors ranging from aerospace and specialty manufacturing to health sciences and education. Using the 4 Principal Mindsets, we have also explored four core organizational types: Entrepreneurial, Competitive, Bureaucratic, and Societal. You may have seen your own organization reflected in some of the case studies presented or with one or more of the core organizational types. If so, the OGI is a tool that could very well support your growth and transformation efforts.

The following questions may support your thinking and reflections related to the effectiveness of the leadership development and performance improvement efforts currently taking place within your organization.

Six Key Questions

1. Is your organization in need of growth and transformation to sustain future success?
2. Is your organization utilizing quantitative metrics to assess its current "ability" to create new value (innovate) and change in adaptive ways?
3. Is your organization aware of its unique cognitive style or dominant mindset, and how it influences its growth capability?
4. Is your organization leveraging system-wide metrics to pinpoint relevant training needs focussed on accelerating growth or strengthening your "readiness" for change?
5. Is your organization's leadership development and training integrated, systematic, and systematically measured to evaluate its impact in support of your business strategy and bottom line results?
6. Is there an Inconvenient Truth at play or being ignored within your organization?

5 Steps to Accelerating Growth and Improving Organizational Performance

Step 1: Utilize the New Organizational Performance Equation (Avoid the Learning Trap)

Put your organization back into the Organizational Performance Equation

Organizational System + Leadership + Training = Improved Organizational Performance

A. Measure your organization's ability to grow and change — identify its strengths and constraints.
B. Identify *who* needs training, *what* exactly they need, and *where* it needs to occur.
C. Design and deliver the right programs to improve your organization's performance.

D. Assess and evaluate the impact of programs intended to improve the organization's performance.

E. Reassess your organization's ability to grow, fine tune, or redirect development efforts where required and continue the *virtuous cycle* of learning, growth and organizational transformation.

Step 2: Recognize that Mindsets Matter

A way of seeing is also a way of not seeing

Understand the extent to which your organization's unique cognitive style (mindset) influences what it pays attention to and what it values. Your organization's dominant mindset as measured by the OGI indicates how your organization thinks, feels, and importantly, how it acts. It is an expression of where your organization directs its attention, energy and resources in support of its vision, mission, and overall business strategy.

Your organization's mindset influences its ability to grow through innovation and transformation. In fact, your organization's mindset influences its perspective on the kinds of innovation needed to support lasting success, or whether it's even needed at all. Similarly, it will influence the kinds of change efforts your organization selects or whether change efforts are even needed or perceived as valuable.

Your organization's dominant mindset will reflect your organization's values and even its unique identity and purpose, such as whether it has a competitive spirit that strives for profits, or whether it has an entrepreneurial spirit that strives for new ideas and growth.

Step 3: View Your Organization as a Cognitive System

Your organization strives for intelligent action

Your organization is a *cognitive system* in that it strives to maintain relevance, while it seeks to achieve its purpose. Organizations are purposeful — they formulate goals and are designed to achieve a defined vision and mission. Organizations are *observing* systems that select, interpret, and act upon data and information in their adaptive efforts. Innovation and change are two key activities that enhance an organization's adaptive capability. Organizations are intelligent to the extent that they are successful at shifting goals, structures, and/or cultural mindsets in adaptive ways to achieve long-term viability and future success.

Step 4: Know that Innovation is a Whole-system Phenomenon

See both the forest and the trees

Given that organizations are cognitive systems, they require systems-based tools like the OGI to first, understand how they are functioning, and second, to know how to improve them in effective and adaptive ways. Organizations as systems require systems-based tools to support them, not tools that look at only parts of the organization; otherwise, its like using a magnifying glass to look at a forest.

This is a key reason why I suggest that innovation is a *whole-system phenomenon*. If you want to improve your organization's ability to innovate and grow, it is imperative to quantify the previously "hidden" and not-so hidden enterprise-wide dynamics at play within your organizational system. The OGI pinpoints the previously hidden forces that both support and constrain your organization's growth capability across your whole organizational system.

Once that is achieved, your organization will be better positioned to design, implement and evaluate strategies and actions that will have greater impact and more lasting effect, given that you will have acted upon a more robust understanding of your entire organization.

Step 5: Maintain a Proactive versus a Reactive Stance

Control the controllables

In a disruptive world, there are many things you cannot control, but you can control your mindset — how you think, feel, and act. As a senior leader, you have the ability to shape the extent to which your organization is ready and poised to confront its volatile environment head on, to seize opportunities as they arise. With better information about the internal workings of your organizational system — to better understand its mindset, something you can control — you can make wiser choices, be more proactive, and take more responsive action. Your organization can in fact grow through disruption.

*****

Throughout this book, "disruption" has been the operative word that can lead to sustainable, groundbreaking, and accomplished outcomes. The solution to disruption is, of course, found within an organization's ability to adapt and transform internally — essentially, identifying one's mindset and making the shift to a more integral, cohesive, and dynamic company amongst all of the company's stakeholders.

The components of the OGI — the 4 Principal Mindsets and the 8 Orientations — offer a straightforward, yet highly sophisticated, approach to determining just where your company needs to realign itself for greater productivity, more inspiring creativity and innovation, more engaged employees, and long-term success.

Now is the time, your time, to invest in the livelihood of your company, management, and employees. Take it to the next level — *Grow through Disruption and Win with the OGI.*

> *"Whatever you can do or dream you can, begin it;*
> *Boldness has genius, power, and magic in it."*
>
> Attributed to Goethe
> German poet and philosopher

APPENDIX A

Reliability and Validity of the OGI

The development of the OGI assessment took place over a period of five years. The initial formulation and statistical validation of the tool was an integral part of my doctoral studies culminating in the successful completion of my dissertation. For those interested in the in-depth series of statistical procedures used to develop a reliable and valid assessment, I invite you to read my dissertation, which could serve as terrific bedtime reading for some.

One of the things are I learned over those painstaking years of research was that statistics can in fact, be fun, which is contrary to popular opinion. That is, if those "stats" are used in the way they are intended, which is to support a researcher's own creativity and judgment in developing an instrument, that is useful. Statistics are not the end in themselves, they are a means to an end.

Validity

People rightly and often ask: "Is the tool valid?" When we speak about "validation," we are asking whether or not the instrument is actually measuring what it's supposed to measure. In this case, does the OGI measure an organization's ability to grow through innovation and adaptive change? Given the applications and case studies you read in this book, as well as others not reported, you could answer in the affirmative. Leaders within organizations who have used the OGI consistently affirm that the tool is an accurate and indeed useful instrument. In other words, it accurately assessed their organization's growth and transformative capability using the 4 Principal Mindsets and the 8 Orientations all embedded within The Transformation Wheel model.

Further, a very strong indication related to the validity of the OGI is the actual correlation with tangible revenue growth the organizations achieved up against the OGI Scoring Index that I developed to assist leaders in "interpreting" the significance of their organization's OGI results. The OGI is accurately indicating an organization's ability to grow as reflected in their actual bottom line performance and results. This finding is, I believe, a meaningful contribution and achievement as a tool designed to accurately assess an organization's actual "ability" to grow at a given time.

Importantly, given it's an accurate assessment of their current state, the OGI has demonstrated utility in pinpointing their strength's and their "constraints" to growth leading to practical actions related to driving organizational improvement.

Reliability

Another aspect of assessing the rigour of a tool is to explore its *reliability*. Internal reliability addresses the extent to which the items and factors embedded within the tool are psychometrically sound, appropriately related to each other within the same factor, and distinct enough from other factors within the tool.

Item analysis

There are various procedures that can be used related to ensuring the items within the assessment have strong psychometric properties. One assesses the degree to which the individual item relates to all other items within the scale, which describes its "item-remainder coefficient"; another procedure involves assessing the degree to which the items within a scale or set of items within a factor achieve internal consistency. This reliability measure of internal consistency is called the "coefficient alpha."

The advantage of these statistical procedures is that they allow the researcher to objectively evaluate the strength and utility of the item set they originally selected to load onto the scale or particular factor within the scale. The item-remainder coefficient or "correlation with the total" allows the researcher to ascertain the extent to which each item correlates with the sum of the remaining items.

The procedure typically occurs in conjunction with identifying the scale's Cronbach coefficient alpha. The value of these two procedures, in tandem, is that they allow the researcher to evaluate how the items within a scale fit together, how they influence each other, and importantly, what the impact would be on the scale's overall "alpha" score if the particular item were to be removed.

Sometimes removing an item will strengthen the scale's overall alpha; other times it will diminish it. It is also important to look at individual correlation coefficients to see how strongly correlated they are to other items; occasionally the researcher may wish to keep an item that is not as strongly correlated with the other items to provide more variation and texture within the factor. And vice versa, to eliminate unnecessary redundancy among items within a narrowly defined factor, which might inflate its measure of internal consistency unnecessarily.

Coefficient alphas ought to be positive if all items are phrased in the same direction. A negative correlation might point to an item in which responses need to be reversed prior to the scoring of a scale or factor. If the alpha scores within a scale are low, it means that the items within the scale likely correlate better with other factors within the overall assessment or with no factor at all, and not with the factor it is intended to support. A rule of thumb for alpha scores is typically 0.70 or above, although some suggest an alpha of 0.60 is adequate for internal consistency.

The charts below indicate the *coefficient alphas* after the third iteration of analysis conducted in 2013 in the construction of the OGI assessment. Subsequent to 2013, the items were further refined and continued to achieve very strong coefficient alphas. Table 2 indicates an analysis that was conducted drawing on the results of one of our client organizations ($n = 95$) where you can see evidence that the Strategic Orientation in particular was improved due to item refinements between 2013 and 2015. Additionally, the 4 Mindsets were further assessed given the inclusion of additional items with ($n = 321$) indicating, again, strong coefficient alphas.

Table 1. Cronbach Coefficient Alphas (Measuring Reliability)

OGI Scales	2013
8 ORIENTATIONS	*Cronbach Alphas n = 330*
Innovative	0.88
Learning	0.77
Collaborative	0.83
Connective	0.86
Cultural	0.70
Leadership	0.70
Creative	0.82
Strategic	0.61
4 MINDSETS	
Imagine	0.84
Resolve	0.90
Analyze	0.90
Align	0.73

Table 2. Cronbach Coefficient Alphas (Measuring Reliability)

OGI Scales	2015	
8 ORIENTATIONS	*Cronbach Alphas n = 95*	
Innovative	0.88	
Learning	0.83	
Collaborative	0.80	
Connective	0.78	
Cultural	0.86	
Leadership	0.74	
Creative	0.90	
Strategic	0.87	
4 MINDSETS	*Alphas 2015 n = 95*	*Alphas 2015 n = 321*
Imagine	0.85	0.90
Resolve	0.73	0.90
Analyze	0.74	0.85
Align	0.86	0.90

The findings indicate that the OGI is not only a valid instrument, but meets or exceeds the commonly accepted threshold for reliability for instruments of this kind. Finally, it should be noted that validation of a tool is an ongoing process. While the OGI is statistically sound in its current form, continued application and research of the OGI will only serve to strengthen its rigor. I look forward to continuing the journey with you.

For those interested in reading my dissertation it is available from:

ProQuest Dissertations & Theses Full Text (1500847861).

Richards, B. (2014). *Innovative organizations as capable cognitive systems: Development and validation of the innovation quotient inventory (INQ-I).*

(Note: I changed the name of the instrument in 2015 to the OGI as it better captured the spirit of the construct being measured).

Index

A

ability, 3–4, 7–9, 11, 16, 22–23, 27, 29–30, 43–45, 50–51, 70, 88, 90, 127, 129–30, 144–46
 proficient, 120, 127
ability measure, 130–31
Ability to Effectively Change, 3, 86
accelerating growth, 144
act, 5, 16–17, 24–25, 41, 46, 48, 58, 63, 69, 145–46
actions, collective, 93–94, 127
activities, innovative, 57, 79
actual revenue growth performance metrics, 126
adaptability, 51
adaptations, organizational, 124
adaptive change, 3, 11–12, 29, 44, 47, 49–50, 64, 70, 76, 78, 129–30, 133, 142, 149
adaptive efforts, 23–24, 76, 145
Adaptive Leadership Styles, 135
Adaptive Leadership Styles Aligned, 137
AeroCo, 121–26, 139–40
Aerospace Sector, 121
agility, increased organizational, 141
AI (artificial intelligence), 28
allies, 30, 64
alpha, 151
Alphas, 152
Amabile, Theresa 39, 94, 96–97
ambiguity, 7–9, 77
Analytical and Pace-setting Styles of leadership, 140–41
Analytical and Participative styles of leadership, 138

Analytical leadership style, 141
ANALYTICAL Mindset, 104, 141
Analytical Style, 138
Analytical styles of leadership, 138
ANALYZE Mindset, 52, 62, 85, 110, 120, 128-129, 138, 141
ANALYZE Mindset and CONNECTIVE Orientation, 141
ANALYZE Mindsets, 110, 138
Anca, 117–21
Anca Group, 117, 119, 121, 123–24, 140
annual creative disruption impact, 28
applications, 95, 107, 115, 117, 149, 153
areas, aligned, 106–7, 114
assessment, 24, 35, 150–51
 organizational, 18
Atkinson, Robert, 27–28
attractors, 93
Ausburn, Lynna and Floyd 71
Australia, 117–18
Authoritarian Style, 136, 138
Authoritarian style of leadership, 139

B

banks, 26, 28
beliefs, 13, 17, 41, 43, 50, 53, 60, 90, 92
BHAG, 119
Blue Chip organizations, 67
BU (Business Unit), 64, 89, 90, 118, 120, 122, 125-126
Brett, 169–170
Building Innovative, 96

Bureaucratic, 65, 68, 138, 143

Bureaucratic– Competitive type of organization, 139

Bureaucratic Organizations, 67

BUs. See Business Units

business, 10–11, 17–18, 21, 27, 29–30, 32, 55, 61, 79–82, 96, 112

business leaders, 10-11, 77, 85

business strategy, 25, 58, 92, 144–45

Business Unit. See BU

business units, 64, 89, 90, 118, 120, 122, 125-126

Business Units (BUs), 64, 89, 90, 118, 120, 122, 125-126

business world, 8, 12

C

capability, 4, 12, 38, 43, 74, 86, 111, 128, 132
- adaptive, 6, 85, 100, 109, 129, 146
- current, 133
- innovative, 37, 76, 87, 103, 107, 117
- organizational, 29, 77

capacity, 4, 37–38, 83
- organization's, 35

CEOs, 27, 31, 77, 81, 91–92, 109–10, 118, 121, 131–32

challenges, 9, 25, 34, 41, 44, 50, 54, 61, 64, 104, 112, 120, 127,

change, 2–3, 5, 7, 9, 12–14, 16, 22, 33–34, 37–38, 52–54, 73–74, 124–25, 127–28, 131, 144–45

change agility, 107, 127–28

change effects, 35

change efforts, 43, 169

change goals, 16

change leveraging, 133

change readiness, 103

change systems, 24

charged exchanges, 85

Charter
- new, 112–13
- new organizational, 111

Chesbrough, Henry 86, 96

Christensen, Clayton, XIV, 6

chronic organizational response pattern, 79

climate, 29, 59–60, 100
- organization's, 92

coefficient alphas, 150–51
- strong, 151

cognitive architecture, 17, 88

cognitive styles, 17–18, 44, 60, 71, 85, 87, 119
- unique, 60, 144–45

cognitive systems, 14, 16–17, 25, 29, 59, 76, 78–79, 88, 145–46, 153

collaboration, 85, 87–88, 90, 106, 114
- real, 85, 87

Collaborative, 114, 152

COLLABORATIVE and CONNECTIVE Orientations, 85, 90

COLLABORATIVE and LEARNING Orientations, 140

collaborative innovation networks, 89, 97

COLLABORATIVE Orientation, 85, 87

College, 101–7

Common Leadership Styles, 134

communities, 88–89, 96

companies, 3, 6, 24, 26, 63, 66, 83, 86, 105, 118, 121, 123, 126, 128, 147
- global, 115, 117, 121, 126
- innovative, 95
- successful, 5–6, 119, 123, 129

company's ability, 3, 78

competence, cognitive, 17, 22–23

Competing Values Approach to Organization Analysis, 71

Competing Values Framework, 61–62, 71

Competitive organizational type, 138

Competitive Organizations, 66, 157

complexity, 7–9, 11, 14, 19, 22–23, 39, 49, 93, 97
connection, 34, 95, 126, 129
CONNECTIVE Orientations, 88–90
consistency, internal, 150–51
ConsultCo, 135–37, 139
ConsultCo's senior leaders, 136
consumer values, changing, 26
context, 12, 16, 21–22, 29, 34–35, 44–45, 47, 51, 87, 97, 119, 134, 139
continuous change, 12, 78
continuums, 61
control, 10, 59, 67, 138, 146
control leadership hierarchies, 68
convictions, 8–9
CORE ORGANIZATIONAL TYPES MATCHED, 65
Corporate Culture and Performance, 93, 97
courage, 8–9, 13
CPS (creative problem solving), 87, 102, 106-107
CPS training, 102, 106–7
Creative, 114, 125, 152
CREATIVE and INNOVATIVE Orientations, 107
CREATIVE and STRATEGIC Orientations, 76, 80
CREATIVE Orientation, 77-78, 80, 105-106
creative problem solving. See CPS
creative thinking, 77–78, 104, 106
creativity, 3, 10, 30–31, 33, 38, 52, 66, 77–78, 94, 96–97, 101, 106, 149
crisis stage, 24–26, 157
Cronbach Coefficient Alphas, 152
Cultural, 80, 114–15, 130, 152, 157
cultural mindset, 74, 81, 103, 110–11, 119, 121, 130–31, 137, 139–41, 146
  current, 102
  dominant, 82
  right, 91
cultural mindset support innovation, 82

Cultural Organization, 69
CULTURAL Orientations, 90, 94
culture, 6, 11, 18, 24, 29, 44, 46, 49, 53, 59–60, 76, 78, 80–81, 92–93, 131
culture change, 53
currency, main, 66–68
customer experience, 119
customers, 8, 25–27, 32, 37, 39, 51, 61, 112, 120–21, 123–24, 140
cycles, 23, 267
  vicious, xx, 37, 116–17
  virtuous, 35, 95, 99–102, 125

D

design, 117, 135, 144, 146
development, 5, 16, 19, 32, 37, 44, 49, 59, 106, 111, 117, 120, 149, 153
Diagnosing and Changing Organizational Culture, 71
diagnostic tool, 3–4, 10, 131
  organizational, 12
differences, 9, 45, 64, 82, 102, 106, 123
Digital Leaders Reap, 157
dimensions, 10, 23, 43, 61–62, 73, 76, 94
disciplines, 49, 67, 85, 87
discovery, 19, 50, 62, 103, 138
displays will, 16
disrupting, 32
Disruption
  high, 26
  significant, 112
disruptive market environments, 112
disruptive signs, 23
dissertation, 149, 153
dissolution, 24, 26, 28
  complete, 26
distribute, 63
divisions, 64, 114, 118–19, 122, 140
drive profitability, 81, 123

duality, 16–17, 158
Dweck, Carol 43–44, 55

E

e-commerce, 66, 158
Ecosystem of Organizational Innovation, 36
EduFood, 109–15, 130
EduFood's growth, 114
Effective change management, 34
Effectively Change, 155
effectiveness, 34–35, 39, 95, 143
Effective organizations, 31, 36, 101
effects, exchange, 124–25
efficiencies, organizational, 120
efforts, XIV-XV, XXI, 4-6, 14-15, 23-24, 26, 29, 35, 49, 57, 59, 61, 76, 78, 82, 84, 91, 94, 101-102, 104, 115, 123, 128, 130-132, 142-143, 145
elements, basic, 51–52
employee engagement, 58, 94, 130
employees, 7, 17–18, 25, 50, 53, 93–94, 112, 114, 127, 147
employment, 28, 95–96
enacting change, 124
enaction, 47–48
enemies, 30, 64
energy, 5, 46, 66–67, 110, 119, 138, 145
engagement, 31, 80, 93, 111, 114–15, 125, 130, 139
  organizational, 120
enterprises, 31, 87, 109, 111, 143
Entrepreneurial organizational type, 138
Entrepreneurial Organizations, 66
Entrepreneurial type of organization, 104, 140
Entrepreneurial Type of organization, 136
Entrepreneurial type organizations, 66
environmental change, 13, 93
environments, 4, 15–16, 18, 22–24, 34, 59, 68, 78–79, 81, 83, 94, 101, 127, 139
  complex, 23

ever-changing, 22
  organizational, 89, 94
epochal change, 13
equation, 99
evaluation, 99, 102, 110
evidence, 29, 52, 55, 151
evidence-based approach, 52
Excelling, 3, 86, 130, 133, 139, 143, 145, 149, 163
execution, 66, 95, 120, 123, 138
experience, 1–2, 8, 16, 30–31, 41, 48–49, 51, 70, 85, 88–89, 91, 101, 105
extent, 25, 45–46, 58, 60, 62–63, 65, 78–80, 82, 84, 87–90, 92, 94, 118, 145–46, 150

F

fabric, 13, 32, 37–38, 79, 83, 104
factors, 10, 27, 29, 33, 76–77, 121, 130, 150–51
failure, 6–7, 15, 27, 80, 84, 91
flexibility, 39, 62, 66, 79
Flexible organizations, 61
flux, 12–13
focus, 7, 10, 26, 31–32, 42, 47, 50–53, 57–58, 62, 69, 86, 120, 128, 132, 138
  external, 61–62
  strategic, 79
followers, 137, 139
Food Service, 109
formulation, 16, 48, 60, 138–39

G

General Electric (GE), 32, 67
globalization, 27, 86–87
goals, 3, 16, 60, 65, 82, 89, 117, 131, 139, 145
  changing, 25
goals of organizations, 30, 64
Granovetter, Mark 88-89
growth, 2–4, 10, 12, 23–24, 27, 29, 49–50, 66, 73–79, 83–84, 109–10, 117–26, 128–33, 136–39, 141–45

accelerated, 26, 32
aggressive, 126
annual, 121, 124
double digit, 124
drive, 4, 38
driving, 135
   generating, 100
generating increased, 127
increasing, 123
influence, 76, 131
organization's, 6, 129, 149
personal, 44
positive, 107
professional, 127, 137
significant, 121
slower, 27
strategic, 140
undisciplined, 5
growth agenda, 125
growth capability, 144
   current, 134
   organization's, xv, 4, 81, 134, 146
growth efforts, 132
growth engine, 75
   organization's, 81
growth focus, 122
Growth Leadership Program, 111
growth mindset, 43, 109, 115
growth rate, highest, 126
growth rates, 73, 117
   lower, 126
   potential, 121

H

Harvard Business Review Press, 96–97
health care, 32–33
High-Performance Organization, 39
human experience, 47, 49
human psyche, 48–49

Human Resources. See HR
hyper-accelerated change, 21, 44

I

IBM, 7, 27, 29, 66, 84
IBM Strategy & Change, 96
Icarus Paradox, 24
ill-intentioned leadership practices per se, 6
IMAGINE and ANALYZE Mindsets, 110
IMAGINE and RESOLVE Mindsets, 65, 135-137
IMAGINE Mindset, 50, 62, 76, 103, 106–7, 120, 122–24, 138–39
IMF (International Monetary Fund), 51
Improved Organizational Performance, 99
improving organizational performance, 144
inability, 22, 30, 37, 91
Inconvenient Truth, 2, 4, 6, 30–31, 33, 37–38, 58, 64, 74, 81, 91, 101, 115, 136, 144
individuals, 6, 17, 36, 41, 43, 46, 51, 77, 84–85, 87, 107
industries, 3, 26, 28, 77, 107, 140
information technologies, 88–89
initiatives, 15, 111, 113, 123
   innovative, 79
innovating, 5, 36, 83, 95
innovating products, 112
innovation, 4–6, 10–11, 27–39, 49–50, 52, 75–87, 90–92, 94–97, 101–2, 117–18, 120, 123–24, 136, 145–47
   associated, 33
   business model, 32
   collaborative, 86, 156
   demystify, 2, 30
   dichotomous, 83
   drive, 88–89
   driving, 3
      effective, 14, 51, 87
   enhanced, 125
   enhancing, 81
   executing, 94

experience, 33
failed, 31, 101
goals of, 30, 64
incremental, 30, 37
industrial, 96
key, 86
leaders approach, 53
open, 86, 96
positive, 36
radical, 86
successful, 29
support, 87
sustain, 30, 38
value, 78–79
innovation activities, 37
innovation agenda, 52, 80, 91
   organization's, 79
innovation catalysts, 96
Innovation Economics, 27–28
innovation efforts, 29, 78, 94
   disbanded, 84
   long-term, 91
innovation experiences, 84
Innovation Horizon, 39
innovation initiatives, 79, 125
innovation laggards, 28
innovation leaders, 35, 84, 91
innovation model, 86
   closed, 86
   open, 86
innovation path, 50
innovation practices, 25
innovation process, 85
innovation projects, 36–37, 84
   empty shell, 36
innovation ratings, 3
innovation strategy, 79–80, 90
   articulated, 94

firm's, 91
innovation struggle, 30
innovation ventures, 81
INNOVATIVE and LEARNING Orientations, 80, 84
Innovative orientation, 82
INNOVATIVE orientation, 80-82, 107, 124, 135, 140
INNOVATIVE Orientation score, 124
innovative thinking skills, 102
institution, 21, 101–2, 104–6
instrument, 6, 149, 153
intelligence, 16, 43
   emotional, 7, 169
   organizational, 19, 169
intelligent action, 3, 14, 16–17, 23, 25, 45, 59, 61, 78, 128, 145
intentions, 7, 58–59, 160
internal focus, 61–62, 160
International Monetary Fund. See IMF
interplay, xvii, 141
interrelationships, 15, 52, 76, 136, 140–41
interview, 4–5, 7
item-remainder coefficient, 150
items, 150–51

J

Johnson, Steven, 86, 88
Journal of Organizational Change Management, 39
Jung, C.G. 55

K

key contributors, 16–17, 23, 33, 58, 78, 81, 94, 128
key factors, 11
key performance indicators. See KPIs
Kim, Chan and Renée Mauborgne, 78, 96
knowledge, 2, 4, 8, 23, 27, 32, 44, 50–52, 60, 66, 82, 84–90, 101, 104

knowledge creation, 13, 89, 125
KPIs (key performance indicators), 12, 131

L

Language of Leaders, 11
leaders, 1–12, 15–17, 23–24, 33, 35, 58–59, 64, 73–75, 78–82, 84–85, 90–94, 99–100, 131–34, 136–39, 141
  ability of, 50, 52
  global, 77
  level, 111
  next level, 111
  public sector, 77
leadership, ix-x, xiii, xvi, xxi-xxii, 6, 25, 47, 50-53, 64, 68, 76, 93, 97, 111, 114-115
  effective, 35
  organization's, 133
  right, 7
  senior, 91, 104, 135
LEADERSHIP and ALIGN dimensions, 130
LEADERSHIP and CULTURAL Orientations, 90, 94
leadership and innovation, 19
leadership attention, 81
leadership development, 143
  organization's, 144
leadership elements, 77
leadership envisions, 92
leadership levels, 30, 37, 101, 119, 122, 126
Leadership Orientation, 91–92
  organization's, 92
leadership position, 9
leadership quality, 77
leadership skills, 58
leadership steps, 35
leadership styles
  associated, 140–41
  pervasive, 139–41
  unique, 134

Leadership Styles to Shift Organizational Mindsets, 133
leadership support, 30, 58, 91
leadership teams, 133
  aligned, 63
leadership team's thinking, 133
Leadership Training, 108
leadership training curriculum, 8
leadership training programs, 100
Leaders of organizations, 2, 30
learning, 9, 39, 44, 80, 83–85, 89, 96, 101, 129, 152
  organization value, 84
learning organization, 83, 96
LEARNING Orientations, 83–84, 124
learning systems, 129
learning trap, 101, 144
leverage, 23, 60, 69, 74, 87–88
leveraging, 61, 70, 75, 101, 106, 118–19, 126, 138
life, organizational, 8, 11, 13–14, 32, 47
long-term innovative thinking, 84
long-term success, 4, 12–13, 16, 35, 47, 50, 82, 110, 128, 134, 142, 147
long-term viability, 2, 5–6, 61, 64, 82, 122, 146

M

management, 6, 18–19, 21, 24–25, 39, 96, 147
managers, 1, 27, 36, 39, 77, 91–94, 113, 140
mandalas, 48–49, 55
map, current state Mindset, 64
market, 8, 22, 25–26, 86, 112, 122–23
  ever-changing, 46
  new, 37
market dynamics, changing, 61
market growth, 129
Maturana, Humberto 19, 39

maximize profitability, 12, 123, 138
measures, descriptive, 130–31
Measuring Reliability, 152
Measuring Shifts, 109
Measuring Shifts in Organizational Mindsets, 99
members, 1, 17–18, 31, 36, 68, 81, 89, 94, 115, 136
   organization's, 17
memory, organizational, 84
metaphors, 14
Metaphors of Organization, 14
metrics, 11, 118, 131
mindset diagrams, 64
mindsets, 9, 37–38, 41–48, 53–55, 59–60, 62–65, 69–70, 86–87, 103–4, 110–12, 114–15, 120–24, 127–30, 145–47
   adaptive, 133
   aggregate, 120
   company, 120
   competing, 18
   core, 44
   creative, 102, 104
   current, 46, 63–64
   distinct, 46
   dominant, 45, 53, 144–45
   employee, 18
   entrepreneurial, 66, 127
   fixed, 43
   future, 64
   highest scoring, 104, 122–23
   innovative, 117–18
   lowest scoring, 128
   operational, 37
   overarching, 63
   preferred, 44
   shifting consumer, 26
   underlying, 46
   unique, 91

mindsets influence, 29, 42, 44
Mindsets Matter, 41, 44, 145
model, 10, 44, 47–48, 61, 75, 86, 92, 136
   financial, 32
   organization's business, 86, 93
Moderate, 103, 120
motivation, 80, 89, 92, 94
   organizational, 100–101
movement, 58, 87

N

NASA (National Aeronautical Space Agency), 52
National Aeronautical Space Agency. See NASA
National Science Foundation (NSF), 52
NATO (North Atlantic Treaty Organization), 52
Natural History of Innovation, 97
nature, 1, 13, 15, 76
networks, 88–90
   collaborative innovation, 86, 97
New innovative business ideas, 5
New Organizational Performance Equation, 99, 118, 144
New Perspective on Learning and Innovation, 39
new products, developing, 37
new value creation, xviii, 3, 12, 29, 109, 129, 139, 142
New View of Organizational Policy Making, 55
Nexus of Leadership, 19, 93, 97
Nisbett, Richard, 45, 55
North Atlantic Treaty Organization (NATO), 52
NSF (National Science Foundation), 52

O

observation, 4–5, 16–17

OD. See Organizational Development
OGI, 3–4, 12, 74–76, 101–3, 105–7, 109, 112–15, 117–19, 121–22, 126–28, 130–33, 142–43, 145–47, 149–50, 153
OGI dimensions, lowest scoring, 140-141
OGI metrics, 102, 119, 133–34, 136
OGI Mindsets, 130
OGI Mindsets and Organizational Types, 137
OGI Mindsets Reflect, 130
OGI Scales, 152
OGI scores, 74, 95, 102, 106, 112–14, 122, 125, 128–29
  higher, 74, 126
OGI Score TIER, 121, 124-125, 129, 140
OGI Scoring Index, 73–74, 103, 105, 117, 126, 150
OGI Tier Performance Rating scale, 131
open innovation paradigm, 86
operating environment, 3, 86, 91
organizational attention, 24, 57, 66
organizational behaviour, 93
organizational changes, 6, 101
organizational conditions, 79
organizational context, 29, 77
Organizational Culture, 55
Organizational Currency, 50, 52–53
organizational designs, 89
organizational development, 11
  comprehensive, 111
Organizational Development (OD), xvii, 11, 30, 111
organizational development initiatives, 102, 109, 118
organizational ecosystem, 35
organizational effectiveness, 34–35, 64, 91, 94–95, 124, 129
organizational enactment, 130
organizational environment influences, 36
organizational growth, 15, 111, 133
  accelerating, xxi

organizational improvement, 4, 110, 150
organizational innovation, 31, 33, 36, 74, 77, 81, 83, 115
  improving, 3
organizational learning, xiv, 83-85, 96, 101, 124
organizational levels, 46, 88–89
Organizational Life Cycles and Shifting Criteria of Effectiveness, 39
organizational members, 2, 17, 30, 36, 52–53, 64, 69, 79, 90, 95, 103
Organizational Mind, 55
organizational mindsets, 53, 58, 99, 133
organizational performance improvement, 102
Organizational Performance Improvement Equation, new, 110
Organizational Performance Improvement Process, 100–102
organizational phenomenon, 93
organizational practices, 78
organizational priorities, 36
organizational results, 15
organizational sensemaking, 93
organizational structure, 88
organizational success, 32, 46, 59–60
  sustained, 69
organizational system, 6, 8, 16, 18, 22, 76–77, 99, 101, 119, 136, 141, 144, 146
organizational thinking, 31, 74
organizational types, 44, 47, 65, 101, 137–38, 143
organization culture, 53
organizations
  bureaucratic type, 67
  codify, 61
  competitive type, 66–67
  given, 88
  global, 143
  healthcare, 34

hypothetical, 65
impact, 70
ineffective, 31, 101
innovative, 16, 66
large, 36, 90
large-scale, 115
manufacturing-type, 120
mature, 66
mid-sized, 115
multibillion-dollar, 27
multimillion-dollar, 27
non-profit, 21
specialized manufacturing, 139
streamlined, 26
successful, 6, 27, 61, 78
vibrant, 142
organization's ability, 11–12, 23, 25, 29–30, 32–33, 35, 58–59, 82–84, 91–92, 94–95, 109, 118, 134–36, 144–47, 149–50
organization's actions, 141
organization's approach, 76
Organization Science, 96
organization's culture, 54, 60, 69–70, 73–74, 93–94, 131
organization's efforts, 94
organization's engagement efforts, 130
organization's growth engine underperforms, 75
organization's growth objectives, 127
organization shift, 80
organizations innovating, 85
organization's mindset, 4, 24, 37, 46, 53, 57, 59–62, 64–65, 134, 140
organization's mindset influences, 145
organization's mission, 3, 32
organization's personality, 44
organizations smarter, 83
organization's success, 81, 141
Organization's Type, 65

organization's values, 52, 145
organizations work, 14
organization values, 45
orientation, political, 42–43
Orientations, 75–76, 95, 105, 111–12, 114–15, 121, 124–25, 129, 133–35, 140, 147, 149
ORIENTATIONS Cronbach Alphas, 152
Oxford University Press, 96–97

P

paradox, 5–6, 8
Participative and Visionary styles of leadership, 139
Participative Style, 139
partners, external, 87, 89
People-Driven Organizations, 96
Perceiving organizations, 15
perceptions, 13–14, 60, 76, 107, 114
performance, 3, 9, 11, 51, 59, 93, 97, 101, 119, 129, 131, 144, 150
  organizational, 100
  organization's, 11, 84, 144–45
performance equation
  effective organizational, 99
  organizational, 100, 144
perspectives, 13–14, 21, 33, 42, 47, 82, 145
  organizational, 83
PharmaCo, 126–29, 141
Philosophy in World Perspective, 55
political mindset influences, particular, 42
power, 4, 50, 92, 128, 147
Pragmatic Style, 138
predictability, 8
premise, 6, 130
Principal Mindsets, 45, 47–49, 60–62, 64–65, 69–70, 103, 105, 119–20, 122, 127–28, 130, 133–34, 137, 147, 149
Principal Mindsets for PharmaCo, 127
Principles of Organizational Culture, 55

problem, 12, 24
problem solving, 44, 50–53, 60, 64, 94, 122, 129
product innovations, 32, 140
  new, 32
products, 25, 31–32, 66, 123
  developing innovative, 120
profitability, 24, 32, 66, 117, 124
program, 104, 111–14, 145
  leadership development, 100
psychology, organizational, 48
purpose, organization's, 53, 68

Q

quadrants, 86
quaternity, 48–49
Quinn, Robert, 61–62, 71

R

radical innovation (RI), 86
rating, 112, 121, 124, 129, 131
Raynor, Michael, XIV
readiness, 3, 12, 101, 131, 133, 144
reality, 1–4, 10–11, 13–14, 47–48, 82, 165
  current, 3, 138
reinforcement, 113–14
relationship, 13, 15, 31, 74, 83, 94–95
reliability, 82, 149–50, 153
Research In Motion. See RIM
RESOLVE, 50–51, 62–63, 66, 104, 110, 120, 122–23, 127, 152
RESOLVE and ANALYZE Mindsets, 138
RESOLVE Mindsets, 51, 62, 80, 104, 123, 135–38
resources, 5, 37, 45–46, 57, 60, 79, 84, 91–92, 110, 119, 122, 130, 145
  organizational, 82
Retail Bank Operational and Digital Leaders Reap, 26
revenue growth, 11, 123, 129, 131
highest, 125
real, 74
tangible, 150
revenue growth performance, 123
revenue growth rates, 117
  expected, 73
  higher, 126
rewards, 26, 50–53, 57
Rhodes, Jerry, xix, 60, 71
Richards, Brett, 169
RIM (Research In Motion), 26
risk, 7, 36, 50–53, 81, 88

S

Salk, Jonas and Jonathan 13, 19
score, 63, 105, 121, 130
  alpha, 151
sectors, 32–33, 67, 107, 121
  pharmaceutical, 126
  private, 32
senior leaders, 35, 37, 92, 111, 131, 136, 146
serendipitous exchanges, 89
services, 15, 31–32, 37, 66, 77, 82, 112, 124
sheds light, 4, 14, 60, 64
Shift Organizational Mindsets, 133
simplification efforts, 128
sized organizations ranging, 143
skills, 44–45, 77, 83, 85, 87, 96, 101–2, 111
  new-found, 9
skillsets, 91–92, 125
Societal– Entrepreneurial type of organization, 141
Societal Organizations, 68
Societal type organizations, 68
society, 13, 19, 44–45, 68, 115, 127, 139
stability, 7, 62, 93
Stable organizations, 61
status quo, 50–51, 77, 81
  organization's, 27

Steps to Accelerating Growth and Improving Organizational Performance, 144
strategic agenda, 79–80, 84
STRATEGIC and INNOVATIVE Orientations, 135
STRATEGIC Orientation, 78–80, 105, 151
strategies, 55, 60, 62, 69, 76, 78–79, 81, 90, 92, 117, 139, 146
  dichotomous innovation, 83
  organizational, 80, 91
strives, 25, 104, 130, 145
styles, 44, 136–37, 139
  adaptive, 134–35, 137
support growth, 37, 47
support innovation, 94
  organizational environment, 36, 59, 89
support innovation efforts, 91
support leaders, 142, 166
survival, 3, 13, 21–22, 26–29, 38, 81, 96
  long-term, 22–23
  organizational, 84
sustain, 4, 13, 21, 25, 30, 64, 81, 144
sustainability, 3, 10, 34
synthesis, 66–68
systemic inability, 6
systems, 6, 15–16, 22–23, 25, 46, 48, 62, 76, 83, 88–89, 93, 110, 138, 141, 146
  complex, 6, 30, 38
  observing, 16, 145
systems-based thinking, 15, 23
systems theory, xix, 6
systems thinking, x, xviii, 45, 86

T

teams, 35–36, 50–51, 77, 84, 87, 118, 129, 140
  executive, 91, 100, 132
technological change, 88
  rapid, 13
technological innovation, 28–29, 32,
  rapid, 81
technology, 5, 27–28, 86, 117
  computer, 28–29
theory, 10, 22
thriving, xvii, 28, 105, 107, 112, 121, 124-125, 129, 140, 142
Tier, 3, 103, 105, 112, 124–25, 127, 131
  high, 103, 105, 112, 121, 129
  low, 105, 112, 124–25
Tier Ratings, 73
tools, 10–11, 64, 88, 101, 107, 113, 130, 143, 146, 149–50, 153
  systems-based, 146
training, 99–102, 109, 118, 144
top talent, 95
training programs, 100, 102, 106
  organization's, 106
transformation, 12–15, 28, 31, 51–52, 57, 73, 76, 107, 111, 115, 117, 131–32, 136–37, 141–42, 144–45
  epochal, 12
  organizational, 110, 125, 145
transformational, organization's, 30, 38
Transformational Style, 135–37, 140
Transformational Style of leadership, 135-137, 139-140
transformational vision, 74, 105
transformation efforts, 15, 101–2, 132, 143
  organizational, 14
Transformation Wheel, 73, 75–76, 95, 134, 140–41, 149
transformative capabilities, 106, 114, 118, 126, 130, 149
truth, 13, 22, 52
types, 2, 21, 43, 65, 70, 80, 82, 104

U

Understanding Organizational Environments, 59
United Nations (UN), 52

V

validation, 16, 149, 153
validity, 82, 149–50
value chain, 32
values, 7, 12, 17, 19, 26, 41, 44-45, 53, 57-58, 60-63, 65, 68-69, 71, 78, 83, 90, 92, 94, 111-114, 127, 138-139
   organization's, 52, 145
viability, 38, 128
vision, 3–4, 12, 17, 53, 58, 90, 105, 109, 119–20, 130, 138–39, 145
   compelling, 7, 137, 139
   organization's, 134, 140
   strategic, 25, 52, 104
visionary, 50, 137-141
Visionary and Pragmatic styles of leadership, 137
Visionary Style, 138–39
vitality, sustained organizational, 91
volatility, 7, 9
VUCA, 7–8

W

weak ties, 88–89
wheels, 73, 75, 134–35
wheels of innovation, 33, 75
windows, 43
winning, 8, 21–22, 27–29, 38, 115
wisdom, 49–50
workings, inner, 5, 8, 10
world, 4, 7–9, 11, 13, 21, 24, 27–28, 31, 41–44, 47–49, 51–52, 115, 118–20
   disruptive, 3, 146
   external, 1, 43
   results-focused, 11
World Economic Forum, 77, 96
World Health Organization, 51
World Perspective, 55
World Population and Human Values, 19
worldviews, 46–47, 49–52

X

X-Rays, 5

About the Author

Brett Richards is the founder and President of Connective Intelligence, Inc., a niche consultancy that specializes in the development of customized training and organizational development solutions in a wide range of industries, globally.

Working with Fortune 100/500 organizations, Brett offers deep expertise in organizational innovation, leadership development, team collaboration, and strategic thinking. Alongside the clients he serves with Connective Intelligence, Brett is also a sought-after industry practitioner instructor at the Schulich Executive Education Centre, affiliated with York University's Business School.

Brett is a leading global Master Trainer in Effective Intelligence®, an international business-based system designed to improve individual and team thinking skills, and system-wide collaboration. Leveraging over twenty years of experience applying the concepts of thinking and organizational intelligence within a business context, Brett has developed and published a comprehensive suite of performance tools, which he provides to a growing number of training and organizational development professionals around the world.

With a long-time interest and academic training in emotional intelligence, he has also served as a Master Trainer and Coach with the EQ-i® (emotional quotient inventory) and is the developer of Emotional Power®, a practical business-based model used to apply the concepts of emotional intelligence in the workplace.

Brett holds a PhD in Human and Organizational Systems from Fielding Graduate University, an MA in Counselling Psychology from Adler University, and a BA from Western University.

To learn more about how to accelerate your organization's ability to grow through innovation and adaptive change, please visit our website at:

www.TheOGI.com or www.ConnectiveIntelligence.com

or email Brett Richards directly at: Brett@connectiveintelligence.com

or follow Brett on Twitter: @BConnective or join Brett also on LinkedIn

International: 905-898-0700

North America: 1-866-THUNK IT (848-6548)

Lightning Source UK Ltd.
Milton Keynes UK
UKHW020936240120
357493UK00009B/49

9 781912 262472